Learning to Read in New Zealand

John W.A. Smith
Warwick B. Elley

Richard C. Owen Publishers, Inc.
Katonah, New York

Richard C. Owen Publishers, Inc.
PO Box 585
Katonah, New York 10536

First published in New Zealand by Longman Paul Ltd. in
1994.
First published in the U.S. in 1995 by Richard C. Owen
Publishers, Inc. by arrangement with Longman Paul
Ltd. for distribution in the U.S., its territories, and
Canada.

ISBN1-878450-62-X

Text typeset in 10.5/12 Palatino

Printed in the United States of America

9 8 7 6 5 4 3 2 1

Contents

Part Two

Preface

New Zealand has long had a distinctive tradition in the teaching of literacy. We have written this book in an attempt to capture some of that distinctiveness, and to show how it has emerged from the insights of a generation of gifted educators. We have assembled, also, a number of studies which show that New Zealand reading instruction is soundly based in credible theories, and that it stands up well to research and to international comparisons.

Education in New Zealand has its share of critics, as does every country. We consider that this book is timely, as it seeks to bring some rationality to many of the debates surrounding the teaching of reading. It is true that New Zealand teachers are idealistic in the way they embrace a whole language, literature-based philosophy. Most willingly admit to an overriding aim of developing in children a lasting interest in reading, and have faith that the requisite skills will be acquired in the context of such an aim — while working with high-interest stories and the activities they give rise to. We try to show how children are encouraged to focus on meaning at the outset and that phonic and other word-attack skills are given their due attention as and when required. For those that fall behind, for any reason, the Reading Recovery Programme developed by Dame Marie Clay, is an effective safety net. The fact that more than one in four of our six-year-olds benefits from this programme is not to be taken as a sign that our teaching approaches are unsuitable, however. There will always be some children who are below average — and these are the ones who should, and do receive a boost. The programme is currently one of our most successful exports.

Of course, there is always room for improvement in our teaching, and while there is no room for complacency, we believe that the New Zealand education system is more successful than most other countries in teaching children to read. How better could we equip them to cope in a rapidly changing world, still 'awash with print'?

In the 1970s and early 1980s, New Zealand teachers tended to look overseas for guidance and confirmation — to the ideas of Frank Smith and of Ken and Yetta Goodman. Now we can assert with some pride, that we have developed in New Zealand both pedagogical and research expertise, which renders the role of the overseas expert unnecessary — though not unwelcome. We have surely come of age in our professional competence in reading instruction. We now have a wide consensus, and a firm base to build on in the future.

This book is written by two people who live in different locations, work in different institutions, and are shaped by different backgrounds. While John Smith has worked closely with teachers and within teacher-training contexts in Dunedin, Warwick Elley has focussed his energies on research in reading, further north, and frequently on international studies. This, the congruence of the authors' ideas is itself worthy of remark, suggesting, as it does, that the divide between theory and practice in this area exists only in the minds of those unable to see how theory and practice have equal and complementary roles to play in successful teaching.

We hope that this book will help the next generation of teachers develop a coherent and productive view of the reading process, and inform anyone who seeks to understand a crucial aspect of our intellectual growth — the art of reading.

John Smith and Warwick Elley

June 1994

Acknowledgements

The authors have clearly drawn on the ideas of many teachers, writers, researchers and children in putting this book together. In addition, John would like to thank Shelley Frew from the Dunedin College of Education library, for her tireless efforts in seeking out reference material. The support of colleagues at the College in clarifying ideas and sorting out computer problems is also gratefully acknowledged. Warwick wishes to thank Gill Ngan and Michele Reeves-Elliot for their very competent secretarial assistance.

T Shirts, by Estelle Corney, was first published in 1983 in the Ready to Read series by the School Publications Branch of the New Zealand Department of Education. It is reproduced with permission.

The publishers gratefully acknowledge the assistance of Sheena Cameron and pupils of Onehunga Primary School, Auckland.

Cover (Onehunga Primary School) and text photographs: Gil Hanly.

Part
One

Introduction

This book is written for students, teachers, parents and members of boards of trustees who wish to know more about how children learn to read. It is not a manual of teaching tips but a considered account based on current practice and research.

The title uses the word 'learning', rather than 'teaching'. While the teacher plays a central role in assisting a child's introduction to reading, we take the view that children learn from many sources — from parents, from peers, from environmental print, from television, from books, computers and comics. Children are active creatures who learn far more than they are deliberately taught.

Why New Zealand? The process of reading for an individual is largely the same regardless of where it happens. An American child growing up on the Californian west coast, a Japanese child in Tokyo and a Norwegian child in Oslo all use the same psychological processes when they read. What differs is the society in which they live, the school systems they pass through, the symbols they attend to and the teaching they have undergone to be able to employ those processes. The New Zealand school system uses some teaching methods unique to New Zealand which are instrumental in New Zealand children being among the best readers in the world. This is not an idle boast — international achievement surveys, book sales and the analyses of visiting scholars all suggest that New Zealand teachers do an excellent job in teaching most of our children to read. Much of the recent evidence for our high standard of literacy was collected in a 1991 article in *Newsweek*. This article began its survey with what it considered to be the best in international practices in education. It opened with the comment that, 'If reading is the cornerstone of learning then the best foundations are built in New Zealand.' (1991:53)

What differs from country to country, and even from area to area within a country, are the social conditions which shape the schools, control teaching methods, prescribe assessment procedures, and ultimately determine the uses to which literacy can be put. The processes described in this book reflect current practices that have grown out of particular social and cultural circumstances. Readers should take from this account what they can apply within their specific cultural and social circumstances.

How are the contents organised?

This book is divided into twelve chapters.

- Chapter 1 (you're reading it now!) introduces the subject, explains the layout of the rest of the book, and asks why reading is necessary in today's world.

- Chapter 2 describes the preschool years where the foundations of literacy are established.

- Chapter 3 discusses the junior school years — the first two years of compulsory schooling.

- Chapter 4 describes the approaches to teaching reading used most commonly in our classrooms.

- Chapters 5 and 6 describe the unique aspects of teaching reading and learning to read in the middle and secondary schools.

- Chapter 7 describes the major theories underpinning our teaching of reading in New Zealand today.

- Chapter 8 addresses the important question of how best to match children with the most suitable books.

- Chapter 9 describes procedures used to assess and monitor children's progress in reading.

- Chapter 10 examines how well New Zealand children read compared with children in other countries.

- Chapter 11 considers the question of teaching reading to Maori children and asks what the school system can do to meet the needs of Maori children.

- Chapter 12 examines two commonly used programmes developed in New Zealand which help children who are having difficulties learning to read.

- Chapter 13 concludes our account by revisiting the question of theory and discussing the criticisms whole language teaching has attracted from some researchers.

These chapters have been organised in a linear way, and for the first part of the book are based on the child's chronological age. The second half of the book consists of a number of important topics which cut across age and school boundaries. Learning to read does not proceed in an orderly nature. Rather, there are spurts of growth, followed by times when the reader seems to make little progress. What are we to make of the nine-year-old who is a fluent reader who insists on reading nothing but Trixie Beldon stories? Or the thirteen-year-old boy who can read fluently but does so only under protest?

For the sake of clarity we have arbitrarily drawn boundaries in the way topics are discussed but the reader should be warned that these boundaries exist more in the minds of the authors and the reader than in the child's world. Learning to read cannot be pinned down and isolated the way a fruit fly is dissected in a scientist's laboratory. Instead, learning to read is influenced by schools, by parents, by peers, by the books that are available, by the psychological nature of the individual, by class and by ethnicity. And we have attempted to address some of these complex issues in thirteen short chapters.

Why read?

Marshall McLuhan considered that reading would be unnecessary in the 21st century. Computer experts tell us that new techniques such as voice recognition will make it unnecessary for people to read. Every recent technological advance is greeted by some self-styled expert saying that this new invention (be it cassette recording, television or computers) will make reading unnecessary. Every expert has been proved wrong. The need for people to have highly developed reading abilities is growing, not diminishing. The level of sophistication needed to read a car manual, a computer manual, fill in a tax form, or read a novel by Janet Frame, is very high. Efforts to establish a level for functional literacy are constantly revised upwards. Currently it is defined as the ability to read at the fourth form level (about fourteen years); doubtless, it will be raised again shortly.

Functional literacy is only one aspect of learning to read. With the steady disappearance of much paid work in the late twentieth century, functional literacy will perhaps be of less importance than reading for pleasure — for experiences which take one out of oneself and open doors to whole new universes. Here are two writers describing the impact books and reading have had on their lives and on the lives of people around them.

Barry Crump describes how his mother read *Coral Island* to the family and the effect it had on his life:

> *to us then, it was a wonderful dream of things exactly the way we reckoned they ought to have been. And for brother Bill and me, that dream came true years later when we lived on a small boat (an old pearling-lugger) on the great Barrier Reef in Northern Queensland. We hunted crocodiles up the rivers on the Cape York Peninsula, caught fish out on the edge of reefs, explored uninhabited islands — coral ones! We beachcombed on Cape Flattery and gathered valuable shells on the sand cays off-shore....there it all was just like we had imagined it twenty years before.*

Here is Dorothy Butler (1977) writing about her granddaughter Cushla — a child born with multiple disabilities:

> *Five years ago, before Cushla was born, I would have laid claim to a deep faith in the power of books to enrich children's lives. By comparison with my present conviction this faith was a shallow thing. I know now what print and picture have to offer a child cut off from the world for whatever reason.*

> *But most of all, Cushla's books have surrounded her with friends, with people and warmth and colour during the days when her life was lived in almost constant pain and frustration. The adults who have loved her and tried to*

represent the world to her when she could not do this for herself have played their parts. But perhaps it was the characters themselves who went with her into the dark and lonely places that only she knew.

Clearly, literacy is essential for maintaining human dignity in a print-ridden society. It is a valuable source of information, of imagination, of security, and of independence. The illiterate individual is at the mercy of the ruthless, and the illiterate society is a fertile ground for the dictator. Reading still justifies its place as the first of the three R's.

Reading is required in many different contexts.

Chapter 2

Early years

Introducing children to books and enjoying them with children seems to be an accepted part of the context of many New Zealand families. We know that pre-schoolers' interactions with books are lengthy and numerous; that they often involve adults; that talk around books is centred on the story and seldom deals with the conventions of print or the mechanics of reading, and that over a period of years children show an identifiable sequence of responses. These conclusions lead us naturally towards a Vygotskian approach to children's development in reading. However, some contrasting research, focusing on other approaches to the early years, will also be considered below. A final section will discuss emergent writing and its links with reading.

What is the role of story book reading?

The foundations of success in learning to read are laid down in the early years of a child's life. How early? Cushla was introduced to books at four months. Her grandmother, Dorothy Butler, writes:

> *Books were introduced at four months, by which time it had become apparent that Cushla could see clearly only if an object were held close to her face.... The practice of using picture books was firmly entrenched after Cushla's discharge from hospital at nine months. Long hours had to be spent caring for the baby and reading aloud seemed a constructive and bearable way of filling in the time. (1977:3-35)*

Dorothy White introduced her daughter (Carol) to books before Carol's first birthday. White describes how Carol's first book was:

> *fated to suffer every indignity that a child's physically expressed affection could devise — a book not only looked at, but licked, sat on, slept on, and at last torn into shreds. (1979:18)*

It could be argued that all this has nothing to do with reading. Neither Cushla nor Carol are reading their books in the sense which 'reading' is understood by the adult world. The books are being used as any other toy in their environment. But Carol and Cushla are engaged in some very powerful learnings when they look at books — or in Carol's case, where they licked them, sat on them and slept on them. To understand what is going on we need to know about child development and how new insights there relate to literacy learning. And, of course, the practice of reading stories at home affects parent/child relationships as well as laying the foundations for literacy.

How do stories assist in intellectual development?

Frank Smith (1985) argues that there is nothing unique about the intellectual skills required for reading. If you can speak, tie your shoelaces and distinguish a paper-clip from other clutter lying on a desk, then you possess the intellectual ability to read. But this is not enough for our account. How does the child learn to speak, how are various objects distinguished from each other, and how does this ability to learn about a universe of things assist reading?

The ideas of Vygotsky are important here. Vygotsky was a Russian scholar who died in 1934. His work, which provides a theoretical underpinning for current practice, has only recently been rediscovered in the West. Four of Vygotsky's key ideas are:

- learning and development are inseparable
- learning is a social occurrence
- language drives learning
- there is a zone of proximal development.

Before the rediscovery of Vygotsky the ideas of Piaget were dominant in educational circles. Piaget considered that development was biologically driven and that learning could not occur until specific developmental stages had been reached. According to Piagetian theory it was no use expecting a four-year-old to understand abstract concepts such as justice because they had not reached the developmental stage which would allow them to understand. Yet how often have you heard a four-year-old say to his or her parents or siblings, 'It's not fair!' — which is surely a cry that justice in some form or other has not been done.

Vygotsky takes a more optimistic view. He considers that learning and development are intertwined and that you cannot distinguish between them. As children learn, so their mental abilities develop. As their mental abilities develop so does their learning. And they can develop faster with proper guidance. Above all, learning is a social event. It does not occur in a vacuum with the child hypothesising and testing in isolation. It happens as the child talks to others, and subsequently to himself or herself. Such internal speech plays an important part in planning, problem solving and enhancing inner control. Thus, children actively construct their view of the world by interacting with others and by exploring their own environment. And central to this process is the child's own language which is the vehicle through which thinking develops. Tharp and Gallimore (1988) describe the role that language plays in thinking as

> What is spoken to a child is later said by the child to the self and later is abbreviated and transformed into the silent speech of the child's thought. (1988:44)

Vygotsky states that: 'Human learning presupposes a specific social nature and a process by which children grow into the intellectual life of those around them.' (1978:88). To pin down this notion he developed the concept of the 'zone of proximal development'. This concept provides an explanation of how learning and development are intertwined. It focusses on the way children advance when a sympathetic adult identifies their current stage of development and assists them towards a higher stage.

> *We propose that an essential feature of learning is that it creates the zone of proximal development: that is, learning awakens a variety of internal developmental processes that are able to operate only when a child is interacting with people in his environment and in co-operation with his peers. Once these processes are internalised, they become part of the child's independent developmental achievement. (1978:90)*

The zone of proximal development refers to the area between the level where the child is currently achieving and the level which can be achieved if there is assistance from someone else. Vygotsky's own definition is:

> *the distance between the actual developmental level as determined by independent problem solving and the level of potential development as determined through problem solving under adult guidance or in collaboration with more capable peers.(1978:860)*

When parents read to and with a child, from a suitable book, of appropriate interest and conceptual level, they have an ideal opportunity to capitalise on the child's zone of proximal development. Here is an example from Dorothy White reading *Toby's House* (by Louise Malloy) to Carol, at age three, and her friend Ann.

> *The first time I read the story to the children they listened quietly, but on the second reading fingers were pointing, questions were asked. They liked a tiny detail, Toby looking out of the window of his house. 'I like that butterfly,' said Carol, distinguishing it from the flies and bees about Garfield Avenue, which she always insists are butterflies. They were doubtful about the frog and the spider's web, but the rabbit received an ovation; each child insisted on patting and kissing the page. The beehive intrigued them, also Toby's bee-keeper's hat. 'Why is the bee in the flower?' asked Carol. I explained about making honey and taking it home to the hive but they both looked rather doubting. (1954:28)*

The story is being read in a social context. Carol and Ann interact with each other and with their mother as she reads. The mother provides a push to further understanding by describing how bees make honey. It is noteworthy that the children did not accept their mother's explanation for this, whereas earlier in the story the children's concept of a butterfly was clarified. No doubt there will be further explanations as to how honey is made. The children did not come to their understandings on their own. They occurred in a social setting (the two girls), and with an adult (the mother) encouraging further learning by her attempts to explain the manufacture of honey. Note also that the interactions are concerned with the content of the story and not with the mechanics of print.

Jerome Bruner, an interpreter of Vygotsky, uses the graphic term 'scaffolding' to explain what happens when a more competent person attempts to expand the understanding of a less competent person. (See Wood, Bruner & Ross, 1976.) The analogy is helpful, as it highlights the temporary nature of the support. Scaffolding provides selective assistance to the child but does not deliberately simplify the task. It maintains the task difficulty constant while assisting the child's approach by means of a series of interventions. Subsequently as the child masters different facets of the task, less and less scaffolding is needed. For example, after a number of books have been read to preschool children they no longer need to be prompted, by the teacher, to begin at the first page or to speculate about what will happen in the story.

Dacre (1992) kept an account of her young daughter's book experiences. Here is a fine example of scaffolding which occurred when Polly was two years old. Polly chose *The Three Little Pigs* herself.

> Polly, 'The pig one!' Polly knocked on the door behind where she was sitting to go with the text, 'Before long a wolf came by and knocked on the door.' Mother read text, 'No, not, by the hair on my...' and Polly supplied, 'Chinny chin chin'. Polly pointed to the first page saying, 'There's the pig'. She then asked her mother, 'Where did the pig get the turnips? From the paddock?' Mother pointed to the picture. Polly said, 'Turnips in the paddock.' Mother asked, 'What does the wolf want to do?' Polly replied, 'Eat the pig.' Mother pointing to the appropriate illustration said, 'The wolf is going to climb down the chimney. There he is.' On the last page Mum said, 'Where is the wolf?' Polly points to the pig's tummy!

Dacre here is providing the scaffolding for the content of the story by questioning Polly, drawing her attention to the pictures and finally by asking what happened to the wolf in the end. Polly responded to all the adult prompts in an expected manner. She enjoyed the story, and part of her enjoyment lay in her chance to contribute and tell her mother what was going to happen next. She supplied the words to finish the sentence, 'Not by the hair on my ...' thereby demonstrating both her understanding of the story and its particular linguistic style. Dacre has built a scaffold around the story which extends Polly's understanding. The child's understanding has been extended by judicious discussion.

In all three cases described above the children are coping with large chunks of text, with the help of another more competent person. The text is decontextualised — the subject of the story and the actions within are not physically present. The children are able to distinguish between the events in the story and the here and now. While events in the story may frighten the child, to the extent that she seeks comfort from the person reading the story, she never confuses the adult with the content of the story. What is being learnt is that stories happen 'out there,' at a remove from reality.

Access and mediation are further Vygostskian concepts which help illuminate the growth of preschool literacy. Access means having suitable materials in the environment which will allow the child to develop concepts that literacy requires. Mediation refers to having someone who is a more skilled person lead the reader through the material. Both Cushla and Polly have access to materials — in Polly's case she chooses from a range of books. Polly's mother acts as a mediator to the story and she has also been instrumental in the access process by providing the range of books from which Polly chooses. Mediation can take many different forms depending upon the family culture. Stuart McNaughton's research, discussed later in this chapter, describes differing mediation practices in the Auckland families he studied.

What is a literacy set?

There are other ways to conceptualise children's early encounters with books. Holdaway (1979) describes preschool reading in terms of a literacy set that children develop as a result of frequent exposure to story books. The components of the set are:

- motivational
- linguistic
- operational
- orthographic.

Motivational factors included enjoyment of books and stories, extensive repetitive experiences of a wide range of favourite books, curiosity about all kinds of print, and experimenting with the production of written language. All of these attributes can be seen in the three anecdotal records. Cushla participated by peering closely at the print and moving her hands; Carol asks questions throughout; while Polly demanded 'the pig one' and knocked on the door behind her in anticipation of the wolf asking to be let into the pig's house.

Syntax, vocabulary, intonation patterns, and idioms all make up *linguistic factors*. Polly's ability to finish the sentence 'not by the hair on my...' shows her ability to use words in the style of this story. Perhaps Carol and Ann were learning new vocabulary — beehive, bee-keeper.

Operational factors include a knowledge of the way stories work in terms of plot, and such strategies as the ability to predict what might happen or could have happened. The advantages of being able to visualise a scene from the text alone without the support of a visual image, is very important for later learning.

Orthographic factors include the mechanics of print — directionality, the concept of a word, a sentence, punctuation conventions and phonetic conventions.

All of these factors are learnt incidentally during shared story reading. Children who are regularly read to will find such factors a great asset in their first reading at school. Should the parents' emphasis on shared story reading shift from enjoyment to formal instruction about print however, in an effort to 'prepare' children for school, story reading would cease to be as enjoyable for both reader and child. There is the risk that it would achieve neither emotional satisfaction nor improve the child's ability to read independently.

All families interact with books — it is presumptuous to think that only middle class families have access to books or value literacy. Many avid readers have emerged from low income families. Clark (1976) studied young Scottish children who were fluent readers when they started school. All had regular access to books and all had the mediation of a sympathetic adult to exploit their zone of proximal development. Clark's conclusions were that of all the variables she studied (social class, intelligence, psychological traits) the most important factor was the parents' positive attitudes towards literacy. Clark describes one home where the father had left school at a young age, as had the mother. Both parents were working in unskilled jobs. Both were avid readers and would sit for hours absorbed in reading. This was a shared experience in which both parents and children participated. Clark considers that her work showed that:

> The lesson from these interviews was a clear one that it is crucial to explore the parents' perceptions of education and the support and experiences they provide by measures far more sensitive and penetrating than social class, father's occupation or even education of the parents. These homes were providing rich and exciting experiences within which books were indeed an integral part. (1976:45)

How much time is spent in early reading?

How much reading goes on in the homes of preschoolers and what happens during the sessions? Anderson and Stokes (cited by McCraken et al, 1985) developed a way of looking at literacy events in the home environment in the United States. The assumption made in this research was that there are many events in daily life at home which influence the later development of literacy skills. Such informal learnings at home provide a basis for later school-based learning which is more formal, structured and systematic. Literacy events were defined in terms of 'the comprehension or production of print in which the child participates or observes directly' (1985:5). Three different ethnic groups, all of whom were from low income groups, were studied. The authors identified 1400 literacy events from 2000 hours of observations, collected over eighteen months. The results challenge the assumption that non-mainstream homes are deprived of literary experiences. There was considerable variability across all families and ethnic groups studied, and the researchers considered that it is not ethnicity or class membership which determines the amount and quality of literacy experiences, but rather the family's participation in various social institutions such as church groups, which are important determinants.

McCraken's (1985) replication of Anderson and Stokes' study in Auckland involved five families from the middle to high socio-economic levels of our society. The children were observed for one day each week for ten weeks. It was found, from 350 hours of observation, that on average 4.5 literacy events occurred each day in each family. The majority of these were reading rather than writing events. Estimates of the length of time spent reading showed a daily average of fifty-four minutes spent reading.

A second study involving only one family was carried out by McCraken et al in Auckland. Several observers were used and the child, a four-and-a-half-year-old boy, was observed constantly in all settings while awake. The duration, the frequency and nature of the literacy events were recorded in this study. The results confirm previous studies. During the week observed, the subject spent 957 minutes observing or participating in eighty-four events which involved print.

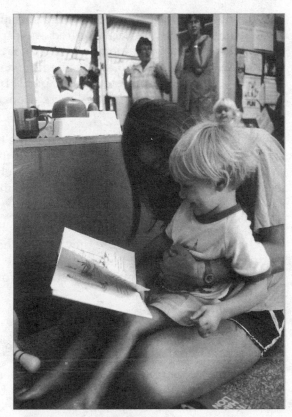

Reading to children is a vital experience.

An average of one literacy event of eleven minutes duration was observed for every hour the subject was awake. These events ranged from participating in story readings to reading labels on toys, reading recipes with his mother, to reading street signs when going out in the car.

So far we have focussed on individual case studies and a legitimate question to ask is, are these New Zealand families typical in the amount of reading that goes on? The net must be widened. Stuart McNaughton has studied story book readings in New Zealand families.

In this case, ten families were studied. All were mainstream middle class families with a mother at home all day. The parents estimated that there was an average of 450 books in each house, 300 of which were children's books. The ten children studied were all between three and four-and-a-half years old. These parents estimated that their children spent an average of 3.3 hours daily on print-related activities. McNaughton tested the children on a standardised test to measure their knowledge of concepts about print, and then asked the parents to keep a diary of reading to children for twenty-eight days.

The results of the test showed that the parents over-estimated the systematic knowledge the children had acquired about print. The parents estimated that their children would be able to identify twenty-one letters in isolation, be able to recognise six words in isolation and understand eight concepts (directionality, punctuation, orientation, etc.) about print. In fact the subjects were able to recognise, on average, thirteen letters, two words and five concepts about print.

An analysis of the diaries showed that during the twenty-eight day period each child had an average of 86.8 books read to them, two thirds of which were different titles. In nine out of ten families the child chose the book to read much more often than the adult. Story books with animal characters were the favourite books.

A picture is emerging of middle class children having many literacy experiences with books and reading before they begin school. In spite of all this time spent on reading books the children were unable to identify many letters of the alphabet or many words in isolation. These outcomes are not a feature of the children's literacy set.

What happens in bedtime reading sessions?

Phillips and McNaughton carried out a further study with the same families to find out what was happening during story book readings. Nine new books were given to the families to be read to the children. Each session was tape recorded and analysed. Utterances were divided into two major categories — book-related or narrative-related. Book-related utterances referred to concepts about the print such as letters, words, print direction, while narrative-related referred to utterances related to the story meaning or content. Both reader and child's utterances were classified.

The results showed that both reader and child made about the same number of utterances per book — about 3.8 on average. Almost all the utterances were narrative related — only 3 per cent were print related. Story reading at home is a shared activity in which reader and child comment about the story in roughly equal amounts, with nearly all comments referring to the story and not to the mechanics of print. The story is being discussed, analysed and constructed by both reader and child. What the book is about is of paramount importance. Phillips and McNaughton describe one incident where the child corrects the mother's interpretation of the story by referring to the text. The mother misinterprets a picture and the child corrects her by saying, 'But it said there was one.' (1990:206) The child is appealing to the text as an authority and is arguing against the mother's reading which is based, in this incident, on a misleading picture.

Although seven of the ten families in this study had more than one child, for most families story reading involved only one child at a time. In only four families was there a story reading with more than one child present. This one to one practice foreshadows the junior school experiences where instructional reading is often conducted as an exchange between one child and the teacher.

Phillips and McNaughton summarise their research findings as follows:

> *Both adults and children have a very consistent agenda in terms of what the child might be learning about how to construct meaning from story books. Both reader and child focus almost exclusively on the narrative. They are concerned with constructing meaning, through questions and statements. The procedures they use are aimed at clarifying the passage being read and integrating it with previous parts of the story or using it to anticipate upcoming story events. From such experiences, children learn ways of constructing meaning using their personal knowledge as well as strategies such as making inferences from hypotheses about written language.(1990:210)*

Similar conclusions were drawn by Doake (1981), a New Zealand educator who studied parents and preschool children sharing books in Edmonton, Canada. Once again, the focus of discussion was on the story and pictures, rarely on the print.

The intensive nature of this kind of research limits the number of subjects that can be studied. However, McNaughton undertook further study amongst Samoan families to see if the literary experiences of Samoan children were similar to those of middle class Pakeha children (McNaughton, 1987). This time, seven families were studied. Many of the activities were similar to those of middle class Pakeha families. The Samoan families read story books with narrative structure to their children more than two or three times a week.

Differences from the middle class families lay in the setting and in the nature of the discussion. Unlike the Pakeha families, where story book reading usually involved only one child and the mother, Samoan families had a variety of readers, with the expert reader often being an older sibling or a relative. Usually more than one child was present. The focus of the interaction was often on giving the right answer to questions framed by the reader.

The Samoan children had all been systematically taught the alphabet by use of a Samoan wall chart. When the children were tested on Clay's 'Concepts about Print' test they scored very low. At age four the subjects on average could identify only nine letters in isolation. However, this result may be more a function of the nature of the testing situation than a true reflection of the children's ability to recognise letters. Had the test been conducted in a more culturally appropriate way the results may have given a clearer indication of the children's knowledge of letters.

Nevertheless, McNaughton's research shows us that, as in American studies, many of our preschoolers have a deep immersion in print before they start school. There are, however, cultural differences between groups, and schools need to be aware of those cultural differences if they wish to build on those experiences. The skills that the children develop reflect family literacy practices and these vary within groups. For example, many Samoan families read the

Bible aloud — accuracy is valued above all else. Middle class families often read stories where children are invited to participate in the reading, comment on the text, and provide creative interpretations. Both teachers and children need to see the relevance of diverse family literacy experiences which should lead to literacy for all.

What are children's typical responses in emergent reading?

Several researchers have made a study of the way children respond to print in the early stages. For instance, Ferreiro and Taberosky (1982) have applied a Piagetian methodology to study the way preschool children's understanding of print develops. They have identified discrete stages of understanding when children are shown a picture with a sentence:

1   Picture and print are not differentiated. The text is entirely predictable from the illustration. The text represents the same elements as the picture. Picture and print constitute a unit which cannot be separated.

2   The print is differentiated from the picture. The text is treated as a unit independent of its graphic characteristics. The text either represents the name of the illustrated object or a sentence associated with the illustration, but in both cases the interpretation is attributed to the text as a unit.

3   An initial consideration of graphic properties of print emerges. The text continues to be predictable from the illustrations.

4   Children search for a one-to-one correspondence between graphic and sound segments. (1982:65)

It is important to note that much of the sequence observed here is concerned with meaning, and only one stage is concerned with letter-sound correspondences.

In a more elaborate series of studies of children's developmental stages (aged between two and six years) in learning to read aloud (within a whole language framework) Sulzby (1985) and Sulzby and Lee (1993) identified eleven distinguishable stages, as the children moved from simple labelling and commenting on familiar books, to fluent reading of familiar and unfamiliar text. Such analyses show development from dependence on pictures to dependence on print, and a transition from oral language storytelling to a form of presentation with the intonations of a competent reader.

The following stages seem to form a stable sequence for many children. The stages could prove helpful to teachers working with children in the early stages of reading acquisition.

Sulzby classification scheme for children's story reading

1   Labelling and commenting on the pictures of the book. No recognition of a story.

2   Following the actions, as represented in the pictures, as if they are occurring in the present, but still no recognition of a coherent story.

3   Dialogic storytelling. Child makes attempts at conversation amongst characters on basis of pictures, but still disjointed.

4   Monologic storytelling. Child tells a complete story, on basis of pictures, but still not using text.

5   Reading and storytelling mixed. Transition stage where child appears to be reading at times, but often departs from the story.

6   Reading similar to the original story. Child appears to be reading using intonation of readers, but often departs from wording of story.

7   Reading verbatim-like story. Child reads large sections exactly as in the text, with occasional self-corrections.

8   Refusal to read due to lack of print awareness. Child believes that he/she needs to recognise the words.

9   Aspectual reading. Child attempts to use print rather than memory as basis for reading, focussing on letter-sound aspect, word aspect, and/or comprehension aspect.

10   Reading with strategies imbalanced. Child uses text and memory for story, and often appeals for help, but makes many miscues.

11   Conventional reading. Child reads independently, using a variety of strategies successfully, with only minimal error.

Regular use of such a scheme should assist teachers in deciding which children need more modelling of storybook reading aloud, and which ones are ready to profit from print-related activities. This kind of research will also help raise our awareness of the important role of illustrated story books in leading children gently into meaning-construction in oral and written contexts.

What about structured instruction?

A contrasting approach to literacy in the early years is taken by Glen Doman in his book *Teach your baby to read* (1964). This book was a popular best seller and is still available from general booksellers. (It is usually shelved with books on how to raise bright children.) Doman advocates beginning to teach children to read at the age of two. (As an aside he suggests: 'Should you be willing to go to a little trouble you can begin at eighteen months, or if you are very clever, as early as ten months.') (1968:110) Materials he suggests using consist of large flash cards each printed with one of the twenty-two 'self' words Doman has identified. The parent is then instructed to proceed thus:

- *Simply hold up the word 'Mummy' just beyond his reach, and say to him clearly, 'This says "Mummy"'.*

- *Give the child no more description and do not elaborate. Permit him to see it for no more than ten seconds.*

- *Now play with him, give him your undivided affection for a minute or two, then present the word again for the second time. Again allow him to see it for ten seconds, again tell him just once in a clear voice, 'This says "Mummy"'.*

- *Now play with him again for two minutes.*

- *Again show him the word for ten seconds, again repeat that it is "Mummy".*

- *Do not ask him what it is.*

- *The first session is now over and you have spent slightly less than five minutes.*

- *Repeat this five times during the first day, in exactly the manner described above. Sessions should be at least one half-hour apart.*

Doman makes sweeping claims for the success of his methods, which he considers should also be applied to brain-damaged children.

There is no doubt that very young children can be conditioned to repeat isolated words on flash cards but whether such knowledge generalises to continuous text is problematical. And whether the child's conception of reading would be either functional or favourable in later years is also problematical. Doman's description of his teaching methods contrasts bleakly with the delightful interactions that White, Butler and Dacre experienced with their children. Holdaway comments: 'If Doman had known something more about the reading process and not been trapped into the traditional fallacy of equating reading with word recognition, the approach may have had some lasting contribution to make.' (1979:59)

Begg and Clay (1968) describe teaching a three-year-old to read using methods similar to those advocated by Doman. The subject was taught for an average of fifteen minutes per day for six months by his mother. His progress was compared with a group of five-year-old children of similar intelligence who were receiving instruction at school. It was possible to teach the subject some letters and some words, to the point where his letter/word recognition score was similar to the comparison group at school. However, once home instruction was stopped a rapid deterioration of skills took place to the point where, four months after instruction had ceased, the subject 'showed no interest or confidence in reading, he could not read two words consecutively from his last text and he could name only six of the eighty-two words known four months previously.' (1968:173)

Such forgetting rates are obviously disappointing, after all the effort exerted. Of even more concern are the effects systematic reading instruction of a highly structured kind had upon family life and mother/child relationships. The authors comment:

> *Difficulties mentioned were preschool negativism, the interference of family life and routine, difficulty in maintaining the child's attention, home discipline problems affecting the teaching situation, and most of all problems arising from a teacher-mother's personal involvement with the child. (1968:173)*

The age at which formal schooling begins varies according to the society in which the child lives. In New Zealand it is five; in Sweden it is seven. Whatever the starting age of formal schooling, the early years build a foundation for literacy where a child has affection, stability, plenty of books, and a willing person to act as a guide through a multitude of stories. This, more than any formal programme of systematic instruction will lay the foundations for a successful and happy reader in later school years.

Where does writing fit in?

Writing skills can develop in tandem with reading skills. And studies of children who learn to read 'spontaneously' at home (Durkin, 1966; Clark, 1976) consistently show that such children frequently experiment with writing at home. Writing without reading is impossible. In fact, writing is the opposite side of the coin from reading. However, it is harder to document the development of writing skills in the home because so much of the writing a preschooler does is thrown away. Young children will pick up crayons, pencils, pens or anything else that will make marks and use them to write. Very quickly the young child learns that some places are not suitable for making marks — 'writing' on the tablecloth, the wallpaper, or adding ones own writing to the printed pages of books usually brings adult retribution. So the early lesson learned is that while environmental print is everywhere — newspapers, books, signs, television — the places that one can write are much more restricted.

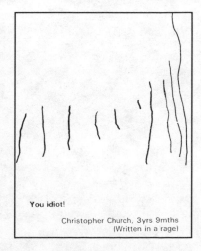

Here is an example of a three-year-old's written message to his mother. To the undiscerning adult there is just a series of parallel strokes. But when Christopher was asked to read his writing, he read, 'You idiot!' As with reading, the context was extremely important. Christopher was angry with his mother and had argued with her. He then retreated to his bedroom, seized a scrap of paper and wrote his message which he then gave to his mother.

You idiot!

Christopher Church, 3yrs 9mths
(Written in a rage)

At age three he has made important discoveries. He has learnt that writing is a powerful way to convey his own messages — perhaps he is working out that writing is a way to convey meanings which cannot be said aloud. Or that writing is a way of expressing strong emotions in a permanent form. Certainly, in his eyes, he considers that he can write and that writing is not just something other people do in books. He has also learnt that, in Meek's (1991) words, message making is different from making pictures. He has a message he wants to convey (and perhaps writing is the only way he can convey it to his mother) which should take the form of letters and words rather than pictures. An older child would be able to use letters that approximate adult forms of letters. To the uninitiated, Christopher's marks are meaningless squiggles but they are based on intentionality and a clear message. He has also learnt that the message can be spoken and read by others — provided, of course, that they can read his writing.

Bissex (1980) has provided a detailed account of her son's progress towards writing. Her book is called *Gyns at Wrk* and is taken from the note Paul left on his door at age five. What is happening with Paul, as with Christopher, is that they are moving towards an adult form of writing without formal teaching. The efforts these children have made to write are not random but are a reflection of a developing understanding of writing. Their efforts have an internal coherence. Meek comments that 'in the case of writing, composing counts for more than copying' (1991:96).

It is all too easy to dismiss children's first efforts at writing as meaningless scribbles believing that they will learn to write properly when formal schooling begins. We should not allow ourselves to be so blinded by notions of correctness, whether it be in grammar, spelling or letter shapes, that we dismiss these early attempts at writing as worthless. Spelling, grammar, punctuation and letter formation — all those aspects of writing that are struggled with in school — will build on the foundations of a child's 'writing' in the preschool years.

Chapter 3

Beginning school

This chapter will describe the changes which occur when children enter school, their preparation for learning to read, the reading materials used, and conclude with a discussion of the instructional stages children pass through, in these early stages.

What is school like for the five-year-old?

New Zealand children begin formal schooling on the day they are five. Legally they do not have to attend school until they are six but over 95 per cent of children begin school at five. Starting school may be a traumatic experience for many children. Renwick (1984) has made a detailed study of the changes children have to adapt to in going to school. For example, when compared with home, school is a far more structured place. There are set times for doing things and the element of choice is reduced. Much longer periods of time have to be spent sitting and listening. While a school may have more art materials, dress ups, and toys than the child is used to at home, these materials are only available at certain times of the day and have to be shared with other children. Then there are the routines of going to the toilet, eating lunch, going in and out of the building in an appropriate way, and adjusting to, or having interactions with, large numbers of children in the classroom as well as in the playground at interval.

Parent expectations also change. The child is expected to be able to do things which could not be done before five. Six hours a day will be spent by the child in the structured learning environment of a school and for five of those hours attention will have to be focussed on cognitive tasks. Parents have expectations of school, too often coloured by their own memories, which may or may not be realistic.

There are major differences in the way adults in the school environment respond to children compared with adults in the family environment. Tizard and Hughes (1984) have studied these differences in the United Kingdom. As a result of observing children and their parents interacting at home the researchers discovered that parents teach their children an enormous amount. What is taught concerns the child's family, babies, household matters and also more general information about science, history and geography. In contrast, early childhood teachers talk more often to children about play and classroom routines, such as picking up toys, listening attentively and following instructions. Tizard and Hughes conclude that children learnt a great deal more in the scaffolded environment of their homes, despite the inherent difficulties caused by other children, tired parents, and a lack of material resources. Children benefitted more because of the personally relevant information that was communicated to the child, the opportunity children have to initiate talk, the one-to-one teaching and the shared memories of so many communal activities during the first five years of life.

In another milestone study of children's language development in the United Kingdom, Gordon Wells (1986) showed that children spoke to adults three times more often at home than at school, and the adults elaborated on the child's utterances twice as often at home.

The beneficial conditions of home cannot be duplicated exactly at school. What should happen is that we recognise that the differences between home and school may sometimes assist learning. Schools provide a larger peer group than do most homes. There are more children, from diverse backgrounds, to interact with, and who will stimulate further learning. We will learn from Vygostsky (discussed in Chapter 7) that learning occurs first in a group and social context rather than as isolated individual efforts. Indeed local research findings from a Canterbury study of children learning in the classroom, confirms that primary school children learn a great deal from each other. (Alton-Lee and Nuthall, 1991.)

As the teacher is not an immediate family member there is usually more emotional distance between child and adult. Preconceived notions of what can or cannot be accomplished, hopefully play little part in a teacher's interactions with a child, whereas preconceptions ('you're just like your sister') frequently limit a child's home learning environment. It is true, too, that teachers have received an extensive education and acquired specialised knowledge and experience of a wide range of children, all of which should help them facilitate child learning. Finally, a school provides structure — children are organised into classes and groups according to pre-determined criteria, whether it be age grouping or ability grouping or some form of social grouping; there is a timetable; and learning materials are organised in a particular way. Such structures are designed to help children move forward, to acquire knowledge and skills, and to ensure enough security for learning to be predictable and pleasant.

When are they ready to read?

Not all five-year-olds are ready to begin reading when they arrive at school. Some have been read to and talked with repeatedly, and have acquired a rich vocabulary and much insight into the basic concepts about print; others, less fortunate, have had little exposure to books, and may come to school with very restricted oral language.

It is worth noting that New Zealand children are launched into reading instruction at a younger age than in most countries. In some of the most literate European countries (eg, Sweden, Finland, Switzerland) school does not begin until the children are seven, and most other countries in a recent IEA survey of reading (Elley, 1992) were found to begin reading instruction at age six. Indeed, US researchers regularly claim that a mental age of six to six-and-a-half years is optimal for beginning reading instruction. Of course, teachers normally do adapt their methods and materials to suit the age and stage of the child, but in a clear review of this issue, Downing and Leong (1982) found that 'the earlier the age of beginning, the greater is the risk of failure' (1982:288).

At present, only a few countries, mostly in the British Commonwealth, promote a start at the age of five — eg, New Zealand, England, Ireland, Australia, Trinidad and Tobago. The fact that national literacy achievement levels at age nine are not at all correlated with the age of starting instruction suggests that there may be no real systematic advantage in an early start. Indeed, there are some indications from IEA surveys, that a start at age five produces many failing readers (Elley, 1992), especially amongst boys. Many teachers believe that it is a mistake to begin children on independent reading of books before they have extensive exposure to story reading aloud and had an opportunity to explore language in its various oral and written forms. A slow start at five years may be worse than a faster start at six. As Clay points out (1991) children who have not been active in exploring their language will have difficulty in learning to read. Such a belief is confirmed by Wells' longitudinal study (1986) of children's linguistic development. Slow oral language growth in the preschool years means slow reading growth at school.

Most schools have, indeed, developed checklists of behaviours which enable teachers to judge whether children are ready to begin reading instruction (Thackery et al, 1993) — ie, whether they have reached the appropriate zone of proximal development for reading instruction.

Typical components of such checklists are:

1   Can write own name.

2   Can repeat simple sentences (as in Record of Oral Language Test).

3   Can carry on a sustained conversation.

4   Can listen to a suitable story read aloud.

5   Knows where to start reading a book.

6   Knows common social greetings.

7   Knows some popular rhymes or songs.

8   Can retell a short story.

For children with significant delay in oral language, junior class teachers will often prepare special enrichment programmes to help develop the desired behaviours. For instance, at one school (Terrill, 1993) children are read to daily in small groups and encouraged to talk about the stories read. The books are chosen to provide a variety of language and structures; they are reread and retold, discussed and dramatised. In addition, the children learn nursery rhymes, practise greetings and other courtesies, and have various shared writing activities. Such programmes appear to be successful in bringing the child up to the required level.

New Zealand reading programmes are developmental in nature. Until children have grown to the point where they can see point and purpose in reading, have an extensive oral vocabulary, and can comprehend and generate continuous language they are unlikely to make much progress in learning to read.

What reading materials are used in the junior school?

Nearly all schools in New Zealand will use the Revised Ready to Read series of books in the junior school. This is a series of readers issued free to schools, and published by Learning Media, a government owned agency which supplies curriculum materials to schools. By 1985 the Revised Ready to Read series consisted of:

- thirty-six single titles catering for the three broad stages of reading development and graded into difficulty within each stage
- seven miscellanies — collections of material of different kinds — graded as above
- fifteen enlarged poem cards for use at all levels
- eight single titles, including one enlarged book for sharing at all levels
- two bilingual texts
- three readalong cassettes (this number will be greatly increased)
- one pamphlet for parents
- one take-home book for children starting school
- one wall chart for teachers
- one classified guide of complementary reading material
- one handbook for teachers.

(*Reading in Junior Classes*:87)

That is the bare bones of the system. What is unique about it is that it is not designed as a finite system. New titles are constantly being introduced. By mid-1993 there were sixty-two titles in the series. There were twenty-one 'big books' for shared class reading, and about thirty audio cassettes. In addition two text-free books were published in 1992. Some schools may supplement this series with others purchased from private publishers, such as the Story Box series, but the material follows a similar format regardless of publisher.

The original Ready to Read series was first published in 1962 together with a handbook for teachers, *Suggestions for Teaching Reading in Infant Classes* (1962) written by Myrtle Simpson. The Ready to Read series and its handbook set a course for teaching reading, much of which is still valid today. Children were considered to be active learners and reading was viewed as a language activity. Teaching was to be flexible and based on observation. Simpson comments:

> *Teaching will be most effectively done in the course of a flexible programme which gives the teacher the opportunity to observe the children at work and to take groups herself as the need becomes apparent. (1962:87)*

It is noteworthy that Dr Marie Clay who has become a world leader in the field of reading research, bases much of her work on Simpson's dictum to 'observe the children at work'.

What is the rationale of the Ready to Read books?

Ready to Read was the first complete set of readers written specifically for New Zealand classrooms. Before then, junior classes used the Janet and John series. This was an adaptation of a British series, produced by the publishing firm of Nisbett, and was introduced to New Zealand schools in 1949. Teachers of the time rapidly became dissatisfied with the quality of the stories and the artificial nature of the child characters and families portrayed. This dissatisfaction, together with escalating prices from the British publisher, led the government, through the Department of Education, to develop its own series of readers. These became the Ready to Read series and were designed to:

1 Offer a series of stories which were progressively more difficult

2 Include New Zealand content

3 Present stories close to the children's experiences

4 Enable children to make use of context

5 Contain stories to be read at one sitting

6 Be 'natural' language texts

7 Provide a national series

8 Provide a model for publishers.

(*Textbooks and Reading Materials*:39)

Each of these eight guidelines has instructional implications. The first one (offer a series of stories which were progressively more difficult) seems simple — learning to read is facilitated by a progression from easy material to difficult material — but in reality this is a complex proposition. It is hard to specify what exactly it is that makes reading material simple or difficult. Is it the vocabulary? If it is the vocabulary then which aspects of vocabulary? Word length is no reliable guide. Short 'link' words such as 'but' or 'until' are often more difficult to read than long words such as 'escalator' — a word which appeared in one of the first Ready to Read books. Is it sentence structure? Again, short sentences may be more difficult to read than long sentences. Goodman (1982) gives the example of 'See Spot run' as an example of a sentence which appears to adults to be very simple but for a beginning reader is far from simple. The sentence is condensed with much of its content unstated. What is the subject? Who sees Spot run? Where does Spot run to? Compared with many elaborate oral sentences which convey meaning with their multiple cuing systems of gesture and intonation as well as vocabulary, 'See Spot run' is almost meaningless to a beginning reader. The written sentence, because of a lack of context, does not provide any real parallels with spoken language. There is no basis from which children can predict the meaning of the sentence.

What about content, type style, layout, illustrations? How do they affect difficulty? There is no simple answer to these questions. Gambrell and Jawitz (1993) have shown that illustrations in books increase comprehension. Children often use the picture as a cue to meaning. But we need further research to examine what kinds of illustrations are most effective. Similarly, we need more research into the effect that type style and layout have on beginning readers.

However, there is good reason to believe that the key lies in the interactions between the materials, the teacher and the child. Experienced teachers have found that good teaching can make books accessible to children, regardless of their technical difficulty. Factors from within the child such as motivation, and previous book experiences, together with influences outside the child such as family background, also have a role to play in determining the difficulty of texts. For instance, Joan Gibbons (1980) showed that Hamilton four-year-olds, who had been read over 1000 stories each, understood new stories and retold them much more easily than comparable children without extensive experience of books. Finally, a good story — one with a well defined story line, clear characterisation and appropriate vocabulary — can overcome some difficulties inherent in the language.

Guidelines 2 and 3 (including New Zealand content and presenting stories close to the children's experiences) are equally important. Reading about New Zealand content allows children to identify with their own country. To be able to read books dealing with life in Auckland or Invercargill provides added interest and meaning. To read about Christmas Day in the sun at the beach rather than sitting around an open fire toasting chestnuts with the snow swirling outside gives our children a feeling that books are about their own world and concern their own lives. The story content can also remind them of experiences in their lives, and allow them to access their own prior knowledge in reading — both of which make the process easier.

'Natural' language texts (guideline number 6) mean that the language of print is as close as possible to spoken language which again makes it easier for children to predict the sentence they are reading. Their natural language patterns have provided them with a template for the 'natural language' texts they will meet in school. Written language can never be exactly the same as speech — speech is spontaneous, repetitive, uses intonation and gestures to convey meanings, and the speaker can get feedback from the listener as to whether the desired meaning has been conveyed. Writing does not have these attributes. Punctuation marks are a poor substitute for intonation. The writer does not get direct feedback from the reader. Writing is more formal, condensed, and less repetitive than speech. To characterise writing as merely 'speech written down' is to commit a gross over-simplification. Natural language texts can mimic the forms of speech but can never become an exact copy of speech.

The Revised Ready to Read series accommodates natural language by using colloquial vocabulary ('Mum' and 'Dad' for the original series 'Mother' and 'Father'), by using contractions ('it's' instead of 'it is' or 'he's' for 'he is'), by using sentence structure that closely parallels oral language structures, and by using familiar topics as subject matter.

Context cues (guideline number 4) are emphasised in junior classrooms. Reading is easier when cues that come from the meaning or the sentence structure help the child fill any gaps. For context to be of optimum use by beginning readers the text needs to use predictable language and deal with familiar topics. By using a series written by New Zealanders, who know children well and who attempt to use natural language, an ideal platform for the efficient use of context cues is established.

The length of the text is important for junior readers (guideline number 5). Too long a book means the child may struggle and lose interest; too short and a coherent meaningful story may not be developed. Books that are able to be read in one sitting of about fifteen minutes allow a child to experience a feeling of success — a complete book has been read in one attempt. The child also feels confident to return to the book for subsequent rereadings. Tomorrow there will be a new and different book. Feelings of success and achievement are being fostered in the child.

Junior readers engrossed in their books.

A national series (guideline number 7), providing it is flexible enough to describe regional variations, is important. New Zealanders are a mobile people. Every five years, 40 per cent of the population has moved house (Royal Commission On Social Policy Report, Vol.1) Some continuity in a child's education can be maintained if there is a familiar reading series at the new school. A series of readers also contains messages of national identity, and shared cultural values.

There has been a long tradition of private publishers supplementing state-supplied books to school (guideline number 8). During the 1960s and 70s Price Milburn produced many books similar in appearance and content to the original Ready to Read series. Sunshine Publishing does the same today. Content and appearance are similar to the original series. These commercially produced books, modelled on the original series, are not supplied by the state to schools — they have to be bought out of school funds.

Here is the text of *T Shirts* by Estelle Corney. It illustrates the kind of material found in the Revised Ready to Read series.

> *I've got a T shirt*
> *A yellow, yellow T shirt*
> *And on my yellow T shirt*
> *There's a great big ME.*
>
> *Dad's got a T shirt,*
> *A big orange T shirt,*
> *And on his orange T shirt*
> *There's a great big HE.*
>
> *Mum's got a T shirt,*
> *A big purple T shirt,*
> *And on her purple T shirt*
> *There's a great big SHE.*
>
> *My brothers all have T shirts,*
> *Little red T shirts,*
> *And on their little T shirts*
> *They have ONE, TWO, THREE.*
>
> *Now we've washed the T shirts,*
> *The big and little T shirts,*
> *And, hanging on the line,*
> *In the wind, we see...*
>
> *ONE, TWO, THREE,*
> *HE, SHE, ME.*

T Shirts is an example of a Revised Ready to Read book. It consists of eleven pages of text with four lines of text and a coloured drawing on each page. There are 112 words of text of which 18 are repeated more than once. The text is highly predictable. The syntax is patterned so the reader can predict the likely pattern after the first page has been read. The text is also predictable from the illustrations which are line drawings coloured in with primary colours. The drawing of the father has him wearing an orange T shirt with ME written on it in capital letters. Everyday terms such as Mum, Dad are used, as are contractions. The text builds to a climax where the final page repeats nouns and pronouns used earlier in the text. The content is familiar to children — T shirts are worn by most children a lot of the time so they can identify with the subject matter. Most homes still use clothes-lines to dry their washing.

This book is intended for beginning readers. It is, however, above all else a story with which a five-year-old can identify and enjoy. The vocabulary is not 'controlled' in the sense of a mathematical formula whereby new words are introduced at a predetermined rate. Instead, the control lies in the repetitive nature of the text which arises naturally from the story.

Each book in the series has a small colour wheel on the back. This identifies the level for which the book is suitable. It is impossible to grade books precisely for difficulty, but the teacher can offset difficulties that can arise when the difficulty level between colours varies. There are nine colours and three initials (S,G and I) which designate the level the book is suitable for, and the uses to which it may be put. The initials represent Shared reading (S) (where a teacher or a group read a book together), Guided reading (G)(where a child reads a book with a teacher in an instructional situation), and Independent (I) (where the book is read alone by the child). The colours correspond to the emergent, early, and fluent reading stages. (This will be discussed in more detail later.) The system is designed to be flexible — a book designated as independent reading for a child at the yellow stage may be suitable as a guided book for a child who is still at the early stage, and as a shared book for a child at the emergent stage. No one book is suitable for only one function. The series recognises that the same book may be used for different purposes and in different ways with children who are at different stages and will be returned to many times — just like a favourite story book.

How were the Revised Ready to Read books produced?

The process by which books were chosen to be part of the Revised Ready to Read series is noteworthy for its thoroughness. The Department of Education advertised in the *Education Gazette* for manuscripts which authors thought would be suitable for use in schools. From the 5000 sent in, 150 were selected for trialling by a committee in Wellington. The selected scripts were printed in black and white, in runs of 1200, and distributed to schools throughout the country for trialling. Trial copies were also sent to individuals and community groups. Trialists were asked to comment on the suitability of materials using a number of criteria — including interest, difficulty level, content and illustrations. The comments were given to district committees who collated the comments and sent them on to a central committee in Wellington which made the final decision as to whether to proceed with publication, modify the story or withdraw it completely.

The result of this extensive process is that there has been a wide range of input into the books. Teachers, children and community groups have influenced the titles chosen. The books give children an interesting and extensive picture of life in New Zealand.

New titles in the series are trialled on a selective nationwide basis. Mabbett (personal communication, 1993) considers that:

> *Trialling reports are extremely useful and usually result in modifications, albeit sometimes quite small, to meet particular challenges. The recommendations for the colour wheel derive from trialling: these are thus not a publisher's assumption, but are teachers' experience from classroom use.*

As well as books for children there are enlarged texts suitable for shared reading, bi-lingual wall charts, audio cassettes which allow children to read along with the story, and a pamphlet for parents.

What are the stages children pass through when learning to read?

The handbook, *Reading in Junior Classes* (1985), recognises three stages in the junior school — emergent reading, early reading and fluent reading (1985:86-87). Margaret Meek's (1982) definition of Emergent reading is used. *Emergent reading* is described as the stage where:

> *the reader learns that a book is a special way of telling story that lets the reader go back to it as often as he or she likes, that the words slay the same, that the pictures help the reader to understand the story, that the story has a shape and the author a voice.(1982:86)*

In addition to this, by the end of this stage, the reader should:

> *show interest in attempting to read the text unaided;*
> *be able to consider what is read together with what is already known;*
> *be able to discuss what is happening and what is likely to happen;*
> *recognise a number of words in various contexts.*

Early reading is subtitled 'becoming a reader' and is characterised by readers who are:

> *using their background information;*
> *taking risks and making approximations;*
> *using the text and illustrations to sample, predict and confirm;*
> *using letter-sound associations to confirm predictions;*
> *using their knowledge of print conventions;*
> *rerunning and reading on when they have lost the meaning;*
> *self correcting;*
> *integrating strategies in a self-improving system (1982:86)*

Fluency is subtitled 'Going it alone' and the instructional emphasis at this stage is on:

> *integrating cues;*
> *reducing to a minimum, attention to print detail;*
> *maintaining meaning through longer and more complex sentence structures, various kinds of prose, and poetry;*
> *adjusting the rate of reading to the purpose. (1982:87)*

These stages can be viewed as the outcome of a logical analysis of the task facing a teacher of junior children. The danger is that these stages may be seen as discrete steps up which children pass in an orderly and sequential way. The reality is that there is no orderly progression — children's understanding of print does not develop in a linear fashion. Concepts that have been learned one day may need to be relearnt the following day. Conversely some concepts may only need to be met once to be learned. What the child learns is not determined by what the teacher does. The existence of a logical description of a teacher's role (to foster these various skills) is useful in that it stops enthusiastic teachers from overloading children too soon with too many concepts about reading.

Clay (1975) cautions that:

> *I doubt whether there is a fixed sequence of learning through which all children must pass and this raises further doubts in my mind about the value of any sequenced programme for reading or writing which proceeds from an adult's logical analysis of the task and not from observation of what children are doing and the points at which they, the children, are becoming confused. (1975:7)*

Chapter 4

Reading instructional techniques

This chapter will describe how a teacher approaches the task of making her children literate. The first section will outline the main teaching strategies employed in the junior classroom. The remaining sections will describe in more detail the practices of:

1 language experience

2 shared reading

3 guided reading

4 reading aloud to children

5 independent reading

6 regular writing.

Some relevant research findings on these techniques are also presented.

What are the main teaching strategies in the junior school?

For the purposes of organising a classroom programme the teaching of reading can be divided into three categories — guided reading, independent reading and shared reading. These categories can be visualised as a triangle, each major teaching category forming one side. The sides are connected to each other and are of equal value. This triangle applies to the entire primary age range — the materials may differ and there may be a change in teacher emphasis but the basic structure remains the same. A balanced programme, one which caters to all children's needs, cannot neglect any one of these methods.

In the early stages, the language experience approach and regular writing have an important role to play. When working with the Ready to Read books, instructional techniques are organised around the perceived functions of the book. A teacher will have a different set of repertoires depending on whether a book is being used for shared, guided or independent reading. While the principles of guided and independent reading are very similar at all ages throughout the school, shared reading is described in some detail because of its importance for beginning readers and to show how the teacher can use it to enhance learning.

(1) Language experience

This is a catch-all phrase used to describe a set of distinctively New Zealand teaching activities very common in the junior school. The starting point is the child's own experience. It may be arranged in the classroom, or on a field trip, or it may derive from something vivid or memorable in the child's life. Through discussion of this experience, the teacher extends the child's oral language and helps record the child's message or description on a chart for the child to reread later — perhaps to a parent, friend or another class member. Often the child will draw or paint his/her perception of it as well. The strategy is described in *Reading in Junior Classes* as 'Experience - spoken language - written language - reading - rereading' (1985:61).

Language experience unites both reading and writing. The function of language becomes clear to the child — what is said tells a story and it can be expressed in sounds, in pictures and in print. And when the child proudly reads his/her own production to Mother, or Grandpa, or to the class next door, the language is more likely to become a permanent part of his/her own repertoire. Here is a chance for real, motivated learning of words, letter-sound relations, spelling, punctuation and syntax.

Sylvia Ashton-Warner's work is an articulate exposition of language experience. Ashton Warner was a teacher and novelist. Her book *Teacher* (1963), is a brilliantly written description of language experience methods used in rural New Zealand. It was the first comprehensive book describing language experience to catch the public's attention and has had a worldwide readership. Ashton-Warner used the term 'organic' reading to describe her overall methods, and 'key vocabulary' for the words that meant most to the children she taught. She encapsulated her approach to beginning reading as:

> *First words must have an intense meaning.*
> *First words must be already part of the dynamic life.*
> *First books must be made of the stuff of the child himself, whatever and wherever the child. (1963:35)*

Ashton-Warner complained that the vocabulary of the Janet and John books she was expected to use in the 1950s in her classroom was genteel and distant from the lives of the children. Her comments about the contents of the readers still rings as true today as thirty years ago when it was written:

> *The distance between the content of their minds, however, and the content of our reading books is nothing less than frightening. I can't believe that Janet and John never fall down and scratch a knee and run crying to Mummy. I don't know why their mother never kisses them or calls them 'darling.' Doesn't John ever disobey? (1963:69)*

Language experience strategies have been widely adopted here and overseas (eg, in the United States, England, Australia, Singapore). For many children this method has been a key stage in their development towards literacy — in both reading and writing.

(2) Shared reading

This too, is a distinctly New Zealand method, developed by Holdaway (1979), and used extensively in the junior school. It can also be used effectively at more mature ages, and has much potential for reading and language acquisition. In shared reading a teacher introduces a book to a class or a group of children, reads the text to or with them, and concludes with some sort of activity based on the story. On subsequent days they return to the book several times, and as they become more familiar with it, the children take more responsibility for reading it aloud in the group or in pairs. Within that bald description there is

Sharing a good book.

room for wide variation. For instance, a more fluent reader can substitute for the teacher, or several children can work through the book by themselves. The book can be shared with a group or the class. Shared reading gives children extended exposure to print in a non-threatening situation. It should be a happy event where the chief aim is to enjoy the experience of sharing a book with somebody else in a totally supportive atmosphere.

A large amount of incidental learning goes on during shared reading. Young children are learning or consolidating basic concepts about print such as directionality, concepts about the structure of stories (beginning, middle, and end) and the relationship of picture cues to the story. They are learning new vocabulary, letter-sound relations, prediction skills, and new sentence structures. They are learning these things at the point of interest, when they are genuinely motivated to learn. The talk, both child and teacher talk, is as important as the text in developing ideas about reading. Shared reading differs from guided reading in that the children are not expected to respond to the text only in ways which the teacher has planned to enhance the child's learning. Shared reading time can lead both children and teacher into many unpredictable, but relevant, byways. It is less explicitly didactic than guided reading.

McDonald's (1991) observations of one shared reading session are described:

> Teacher (*holds the book up to the children so they can see the text*):*He's probably meowing quite loudly. How would I guess that?*
> Gemma: *Because it's got, because it's got ...excremation...*
> Sally: *Extremation.*
> Sue: *Extremation marks.*
> Teacher: *Oh, good on you. The exclamation marks (teacher shows children the picture that accompanies the text).*
> Teacher: *Who do you think this is, Nicole? This lady here?*
> Nicole: *Mummy.*
> Teacher: *It's Mum! Do you think she will feed the cat? Do you think she will, Jackie?*
> Jackie: *No.*
> Teacher: *Let's find out (teacher and children read the text in unison).*
> John: *Hey — there's talking marks?*
> Teacher: *Why are there talking marks?*
> John: *'Cause the cat's going meow, meow, meow.*
> Teacher: *No, where Mum's talking they've got talking marks...Who's this man going to be? (Shows the picture page to the children)*
> Jan: *Grandad.*
> Teacher: *Grandad? Could be.*
> Simon: *Grandpop?*
> George: *Uncle.*
> Teacher: *What makes you think it's uncle, George?*
> George: *Because I've heard the story before.(1991:3)*

What is happening here is that the teacher is trying to get the children to predict what will happen in the story. The children are responding from a variety of viewpoints — Gemma and Sally are responding on the basis of punctuation marks in the text, Jan and Simon make predictions after looking at the picture and George draws on knowledge gained from a previous reading. McDonald describes the process as: 'the written word becomes the focus of a shared group activity, transforming the text into a classroom dialogue by means of a structured negotiation between the teacher and the children.' (1991:3) Children may each take different understandings about print and the story from the session.

How effective is shared reading in helping children improve their reading? A Christchurch study conducted by Elley (1985) in seventy-four primary school classrooms showed that teachers who produced the largest gains in reading achievement over a school year spent more time on shared reading and less time on pupils reading aloud. Also, teachers whose children showed strongest positive interest in reading spent more time on shared reading, listening posts, teacher reading aloud and pupil silent reading.

The Fiji Book Flood Study carried out by Elley and Mangubhai (1983) in Fiji rural schools was designed to evaluate the shared reading method and the sustained silent reading method (SSR) in an ESL situation, just as the children started their schooling in English (Years 4 and 5). Half the Book Flood teachers were trained over three days to implement the shared reading method, the other half followed the SSR approach, with occasional storyreading by the teacher. They had no special training. The control group teachers had a one-day workshop on their structured language programme (Tate Language Syllabus).

Teachers in the eight Book Flood schools were given 250 books, in sets of about fifty, over a period of two years. Funds were raised from charities, and the books were purchased from New Zealand, the United States or the United Kingdom, as there was very little local indigenous children's literature. Books were kept in classrooms, in book corners or classroom libraries, or on display.

Time spent on teaching English — reading, writing, grammar — was standardised. The researchers visited the schools about every two months to ensure that teachers were administering the programmes as intended, to distribute books and to observe lessons and student's work.

At the end of both years, all students were tested by outside educators on standard tests of reading, listening, writing, vocabulary and grammar. Access was also gained to the students' results in the national Fiji Intermediate Examination, taken in Year 6. The results of the evaluation were consistent and striking. After one year, the two Book Flood groups (Shared Reading and Silent Reading) had improved at twice the normal rate in reading comprehension. They were also well ahead of the control groups in each test of reading, listening and grammar in both grade levels but less so in oral language. After two years the gains had increased in all language areas and the results of the national examinations were very exciting. The shared reading group had actually doubled their usual pass rate in English so that twice as many children left the village that year to attend high school in town. One of these small schools had the second highest performance level in Fiji, to the delight of their staff.

Further research on the benefits of this strategy have been conducted in Singapore primary schools, also with very pleasing results. Follow-up studies showed that the Singapore pupils who followed a book-based programme, with daily shared reading and language experience, produced large gains in reading, writing and language (Elley, 1991). Singapore teachers who were initially sceptical of an approach based on enjoyable experiences with stories, rapidly changed their views when they saw the benefits of more positive attitudes and enhanced learning on the part of their children. Furthermore, these gains have been reflected in the recent IEA survey of reading-literacy. Singapore, which has adopted shared reading nationally, was the only country where children learning to read in their second language produced high mean scores that were well above the international averages.

In another study conducted in the Pacific Island of Niue, Peter De'Ath (1980), a gifted New Zealand reading teacher, developed a set of simple readers in English modelled on the New Zealand Ready to Read series. He then trained six local teachers (of Year 3) to teach these books by the shared reading method. Although the children in these six schools were learning in their second language, they absorbed the language of the books very quickly and gained much pleasure from the stories. A formal evaluation after twelve months on the shared reading programme showed that the students were learning word recognition, oral language and reading comprehension at twice the rate of control groups of similar age and ability (Elley, 1980). The control groups were learning the same skills from the widely-used Tate Oral Language Syllabus with its accompanying reading books, produced by the South Pacific Commission (1971). Collectively, these evaluations of shared reading suggest that it contributes much to children's literacy.

Guided reading, reading to children and independent reading form the core activities in effective middle school reading programmes. Shared reading, as practised in many junior classrooms, is used less often with children in the middle school who are progressing satisfactorily.

(3) Guided silent reading

Guided silent reading is one of the main teaching techniques used at all levels of the school, from new entrant through to Form 2 classes. The basis of guided reading is a teacher and a child or a group of children reading a story together silently, with periodic discussion. The sessions follow a simple format — an introduction, followed by supported reading and sometimes a conclusion with some form of follow-up activity. The text is introduced to the reader who is then 'guided' through it. Guiding can consist of asking a series of questions and getting the children to answer by reading silently through, or referring to the text and reading sections aloud, and then discussing their answers with the group. Effective guided reading lessons involve the children in reading and discussing as much as possible. In line with Vygotskian thinking, the teacher provides support by assisting the reader to clarify meaning through utilising problem solving strategies. The teacher is able to keep an informal check on each child's progress by observing the strategies the reader is using. Thus the teacher plays a key role in guided reading.

The children taking part in the session can be a group formed on the basis of achievement level, interest, friendship or they may be brought together because all those particular children share a common need to work through a particular story. Grouping should be flexible and varied. Grouping allows children to support each other in reading and feel part of a community of readers. It also allows for the efficient use of a teacher's time. Alternatively, guided silent reading can take place between the teacher and one child depending on the classroom organisation and the needs of the child.

The importance of pre-reading discussion

Strong evidence supports the vital role that pre-reading discussion plays in helping children's oral reading. Wong and McNaughton (1980) worked with a low progress child aged seven-and-a-half-years. When he was given reading books appropriate for a child who had been at school for two and a half years he read with only 70 per cent accuracy. There was little self-correction and his errors were often senseless and inappropriate to the context. However, his reading changed dramatically when the story was discussed with him before reading it. The discussions were described by Wong and McNaughton:

> concepts, events, actions and vocabulary were highlighted in the conversation (for example, what would be a good thing to do if you couldn't keep warm in a cave?) which lasted less than five minutes. Words in the text were not identified. (1980:41)

Over the next four sessions the boy read with 90 per cent accuracy and self corrected one in every two errors. When the researchers stopped pre-discussion there was a return to previous levels of responding and when the discussion was reinstated the child's performance increased dramatically. This research has profound implications for classroom practices by showing that children's oral reading accuracy improves if they have activated relevant ideas, before they begin to read.

The form of pre-reading discussion is important. It should be a general discussion of the concepts in the story and not a direct teaching session where vocabulary is pre-taught without any context. An emphasis should be placed on context and relating the story to the child's own experiences and knowledge. To use Ausubel's appropriate terminology, 'advance organisers' are being set up. Children are organising relevant background information in advance. Bruner's term 'scaffolding' is an apt summary of the process because a more skilled person is assisting a less skilled person to 'mediate' the relevant ideas and so helping the reader in understanding a text. The focus of the discussions in the Wong and McNaughton study was on the story and not on the mechanics of print. Letters, words and sounds were not pre-taught in the discussion session. After the reading it may be of some use to draw the reader's attention to some salient features of the print, provided it does not interfere with the child's understanding of the meaning of the story.

How is the story divided up?

The material to be read should be broken into logical chunks for the children to read. The size of the chunks depends on the nature of the material, the purpose of the reading and the age of the reader. For a young reader at the emergent reading stage, two pages of a Ready to Read book will be a sufficient length, whereas for a fluent twelve-year-old reader an entire story may be read in one chunk. Non-fiction material may possibly be read in small chunks whereas a sure road to the destruction of a good story is fragmenting it into separate paragraphs to be read in a guided reading session. While the paramount aim of reading for the children is to gain meaning, the teacher may have particular aims for the session. For example, she may wish to strengthen the steps her group of six-year-olds are taking towards silent reading and will suggest strategies the children can employ to read silently. The children will need to read longer, connected passages to develop the necessary skills to achieve this. Conversely a teacher may wish to check on the way Form 2 children can relate details to the main idea in a non-fiction article. She may ask the children to read the relevant pages and then read aloud the details that elaborate the main ideas in the story.

What is the role of follow-up activities?

Not every guided reading lesson needs to conclude with follow-up activities. Often reading the story is sufficient in itself and does not need to be supplemented with any other activity. However, follow-up activities are sometimes needed as a classroom management tool which will give the children purposeful independent activities leaving the teacher free to attend to the needs of other children in her class. The range and quality of follow-up activities depend on the teacher's understanding of the reading process and her creativity in designing activities that complement the learning that has taken place in the guided reading session. Activities following a guided reading lesson should draw the child back to the text and reinforce the major learning points of the guided session. Typical activities might include responding to written questions, cloze exercises, role plays, vocabulary extension, reading aloud in pairs, or rewriting of the story.

How common is guided reading?

In Henson's (1991) survey of seventy-seven middle school teachers he reported that 67 per cent regularly used some form of guided silent reading although the lessons also allowed for some oral reading. Those who did not use it, often had individual programmes with conferencing. Elley (1985) reported that from a sample of seventy-five Canterbury teachers, guided silent reading took up an average of thirty-eight minutes of class time a week. Clearly, it is a major component of New Zealand reading programmes.

(4) Reading aloud to children

This activity usually involves the whole class and is a daily part of the programme. It is not an activity confined to junior classes. Its chief virtues are that it provides modelling of appropriate reading behaviour, enjoyment of good literature and exposure to different genres.

New Zealand teachers spend much time reading aloud to their classes. Elley (1985) claims that teachers spend approximately twenty to twenty-five minutes each day reading aloud to children, either in recreational reading or shared reading. His claim is based on a survey of seventy-five teachers who taught at levels ranging from Standard 2 to Form 2 conducted in Canterbury primary schools. Henson's 1991 survey confirmed Elley's findings in that nearly all the teachers questioned said they read daily to their class.

The IEA survey revealed that New Zealand teachers read aloud more often than teachers in other countries (Wagemaker, 1993). This activity directly correlates with high achievement in reading. International studies of teachers' behaviour suggest this is an unusual allotment of time on the part of New Zealand teachers, yet the practice of reading aloud is more characteristic of high achieving countries than low-achieving countries in analyses of reading/ literacy levels (Elley, 1992).

Specific gains from reading to children

What is the rationale for spending so much time reading to children? Is it merely a frill to amuse a bored class, or does it have real benefits for children? Holdaway (1979) spells out many benefits that follow from being read to. Adopting his views, and elaborating on them, we can list the following advantages:

1 Children are more likely to develop a love of good books and good literature if the reading is done well.

2 Children gain practice in visualising events and objects which are removed in time and place. This 'decontextualising' ability, to think about things out of their context, is an important element in much school work.

3   Children extend their imagination as they are led to picture other possible worlds.

4   Children expand their vocabulary and understanding of good sentence structure.

5   Children develop a familiarity with story grammar. They understand the common sequence of setting, characters, plot, climax, resolution, and are thus better able to predict and appreciate new stories.

These benefits are based on observation and logic. How well do they translate into hard evidence? Several studies have been conducted to assess the impact of regular story reading on children. For instance, Elley (1989) found that eight- and nine-year-old New Zealand children typically showed a 15-20 per cent gain in vocabulary from stories they heard read aloud. When the teacher attempted to explain or illustrate the target words in passing, the gains rose to 40 per cent. A study by Feitelson et al (1986) with Israeli first graders showed significant gains in comprehension, retelling, vocabulary range, sentence length and understanding of story structure as a result of listening to a story twenty minutes daily for five months. Similar effects have been found by Ricketts in Fiji (1983), by Morrow in the United States (1992) and by Phillips in Newfoundland (1989). There is much reason to believe then, that children learn new language readily by listening to a good story. While those who regularly read to children require little confirmation of the benefits of reading to children, there is a need for more hard data on these claimed advantages.

(5) Independent reading

Independent reading is an activity in which children, alone or with friends, read their own self-selected books during a set period of time each day. It is similar to the recreational reading done by adults and provides a time for children to enjoy reading and to practise the skills learnt in guided reading sessions. All children must be given time for independent reading — from the new entrant, clutching a browsing box which contains a collection of picture books and stories she has already read several times, to the Form 2 child, with a taste for fantasy reading such as *Under the Mountain* (Maurice Gee). Often, independent reading takes place daily during uninterrupted sustained silent reading time, discussed in detail below.

Silent reading by children

Uninterrupted Sustained Silent Reading (USSR) is the name often given to the widespread New Zealand practice in which everybody in a class (including the teacher) reads silently from self-selected books. The programme has attracted a variety of names (Drop Everything And Read [DEAR], Sustained Silent Reading [SSR]), but all apply to a similar procedure. The key components are that all students in a class and their teacher read silently for a set period of time each day, from their own book, chosen by themselves. The time should be used for reading only — changing books, completing exercises or any other activities should be banned. To ensure that the sessions are conducted in the right spirit, there are no follow-up activities or questions at the end of the session. USSR is an individual activity which provides a chance for children to practise previously learnt strategies.

Henson found that 87 per cent of the teachers he surveyed had regular silent reading sessions lasting between ten and thirty minutes (1991:8). Elley (1985) in his study of Canterbury teachers found that an average of fifty minutes a week was spent on silent reading by children. Again, such figures indicate more use of independent reading in New Zealand classrooms then in other countries (Wagemaker, 1993). In view of an international trend towards less reading out of school, as television and computers take up more of children's leisure time, it is important that schools maintain this practice.

How beneficial is silent reading for children?

The value of silent reading is widely accepted by teachers. How effective is such regular silent reading in raising children's achievement levels in reading? Numerous research studies can be quoted to show that it is a very useful way of using student time.

Diary studies of time allotments by American children, conducted by Anderson et al (1988) and by Taylor et al (1990), demonstrate that middle-school children who spend more time reading, in or out of school, show greater gains in reading achievement levels. Time spent watching television was consistently counterproductive. Similar findings have emerged from a Christchurch study of eleven to twelve year olds by Rogers (1994). Frequent readers showed higher reading achievement, and no children achieved well in the absence of frequent reading. Again, television viewing was negatively related to reading levels.

In an experimental study of Spanish-speaking American pupils, Schon et al (1982) found that children who were reading silently in Spanish, daily, showed significantly greater gains than control groups in both Spanish comprehension and vocabulary, and with no loss to their English reading development. The Fiji Book Flood, summarised above, also showed clear benefits for regular silent reading. Further studies of this sort are summarised by Krashen (1988). More recently, the IEA Reading Literacy study, conducted in thirty-two countries, confirmed internationally the value of silent reading (Elley, 1992). There is strong support in these research investigations for the old adage forcefully promoted by Frank Smith (1975) and so widely accepted by New Zealand teachers, that we do learn to read by reading.

Why is it so effective? Wilkinson and Anderson (1992) examined how silent reading in small group lessons influenced children's learning. They identified three factors that made silent reading more efficient than oral reading. The first factor was pacing. Silent reading is normally faster than oral reading so more words per minute are read during silent reading. If reading is improved by practice then this is a real advantage. Student attention was the second factor. During silent reading all students in a group are directly engaged in reading. This contrasts with group oral reading where there are interruptions with children calling out and the oral errors are obvious and overtly corrected. The third factor was an emphasis on story meaning. During silent reading, the reader's attention is focused on gaining meaning from the page rather than saying the words aloud for an audience. Too often, oral reading sessions become elocution performances where the readers struggle to vary their voices for a bored audience which often has a copy of the story in front of them and has already read the story.

The conclusion that Wilkinson and Anderson reached from their study is that the benefits of silent reading are socially constructed. That is, in a group situation, group membership, the role of the teacher and the story content all interact and influence a reader's understanding. Interestingly, the authors comment that silent reading is more beneficial than oral reading even for children who are not yet fluent readers.

Research evidence also shows that there is a high amount of on-task behaviour during SSR and that when the teacher reads from his or her own book the amount of on-task behaviour increases. In a series of studies, Wheldall and Entwistle (1988) showed that when children read teacher-selected material and the teacher did not read silently with the class, on-task behaviour was only 50 per cent, whereas when children read self-selected books and the teacher read silently along with the class, on-task behaviour rose to 73 per cent.

This research shows how powerful role models are in learning to read. Indeed, social learning theorists such as Bandura, believe that children learn most of their behaviour through modelling. With USSR it is a case of 'do as I do' from the teacher rather than a case of 'do as I say'.

New Zealand research on USSR was conducted by Pluck, Ghafari, Glynn and McNaughton (1984). Ten children, aged between eight and nine years, were studied. Five were high achieving readers and five were struggling with reading. During the baseline conditions of the study the children were observed while the teacher was seated at a desk and worked on a variety of administrative tasks. In the experimental phase the teacher, as well as the children, read from books. Both low and high achievers made gains in the amount of time spent on task when reading under the experimental conditions, with the greatest gains being made by the low achievers. While the teacher was reading, the percentage of time on task for low achievers rose from a mean of 31 per cent to a mean of 65 per cent. The gains were somewhat less striking for high achievers, changing from an average of 69 per cent during baseline to an average of 85 per cent during modelling conditions.

The implications from this research are that it is vital that teachers read and are seen reading by their class. We should vigorously challenge the perception of teaching, whereby a teacher sitting at a desk, reading, while the class also reads, is not considered to be 'working'. McNaughton comments that 'if a valued person is observed at least occasionally to be functionally engaged in the activity, then the probability of independent reading is increased.' (1990:142) In an era when children are exposed to so many counter-attractions out of school — television, computer games, videos, sports — it is all the more important that schools set aside time for children to devote themselves exclusively to reading, without distraction.

(6) The role of writing

Where does writing fit into learning to read? It is useful to think of reading and writing as two subsets of a larger concept, literacy. There is a reciprocal interaction between reading and writing which benefits both. Both require the structuring of letters, words and sentences. Both depend on what the child knows about the world. We cannot write without a subject, just as we cannot read without reading about something. Both processes rely on some visual input.

There are also significant differences. Writing is a sequential process where letters and words are set down in linear order on a page. Every letter is needed. Reading is not such a linear process. Eye movement studies have shown that the fixations of an eye as it moves along a line of print are not a steady progression from the beginning of the line to the end, but rather a series of jumps from salient points on the line with many regressions. The reader responds to shapes and fragments; the writer must record every letter. In writing there are fixed conventions about spelling which require precision and conscious effort by the writer. Reading is not a word-by-word process and the reader does not identify every word on a page (Smith, 1975). Writing relies heavily on punctuation and capitalisation to convey the aspects of meaning which gesture and intonation convey in speech.

Writing is a regular occurrence in New Zealand junior classes. This is important as learning to write at the same time as one learns to read adds much to the knowledge one needs to become a fluent reader. As they labour over producing their first stories, beginning writers are learning about the conventions of print (directionality, punctuation, letter-sound relationships), an understanding of which is vital for fluent reading. In a whole language programme, writing plays a key role in helping a child match symbol with sound. As Clay puts it (1991) the child must break down the task to its smallest segments while at the same time synthesising them into words and sentences. This is a crucial learning time.

Clay (1975) has made a close analysis of five-year-olds' early writing behaviours and found interesting progressions in their efforts. It has become clear that writing plays a big role in helping children organise their reading behaviour. For instance, after six months at school 50 per cent of children still have difficulty understanding the concepts of 'letter' and 'word'. Writing helps them clarify these concepts. It is not surprising that writing activities are a daily feature of the junior classroom, and that they figure prominently in many remedial reading programmes.

Chapter 5

The middle years

This chapter will discuss the aims teachers of middle school children hold for their teaching of reading and ways in which they can be achieved. This includes a discussion of the reading materials children use in the middle school; how children's comprehension strategies can be developed by an understanding of the transactional theory of comprehension and a description of reciprocal teaching techniques and supporting research. The final section outlines Holdaway's procedure for individualising instruction, and refers to other promising leads in the research.

The middle years straddle the ages seven to twelve. These are the years when children are in the standard classes and in many cases include two years in intermediate schools. The pattern of schooling that children have become used to in their first two years continues largely unchanged, with a healthy emphasis on active learning. However, many classes are made up from cross-age grouping of children. Sixty-one per cent of nine-year-olds in 1993 were taught in composite classes (Wagemaker, 1993) in which one teacher teaches all the major curriculum areas to children from at least two class levels eg, Standard 2 and Standard 3. In small rural schools all class levels may be found in one room. About half of our eleven- and twelve-year-old children go to intermediate schools and the changes they face at that point — wearing uniforms, specialist teachers for art, home economics, woodwork and metal work — are harbingers of greater changes they will meet at secondary school.

What are the challenges of reading in the middle school?

There are changes in the way the teaching of reading is approached in these middle years. Children are exposed to a greater variety of materials eg, more independent reading and expository text; new forms of assessment eg, group standardised tests; and teaching procedures such as visits to the school library. In some cases, particularly towards the end of the primary years, less emphasis might be placed on teaching reading, in the often mistaken view that as the children can already read fluently, the classroom programme does not need to include specific sessions on reading. There is still much help and guidance that teachers can offer. Differences in attainment become more apparent in these years and there is a constant challenge to teachers to provide appropriate instruction for all children at many levels of ability. According to standardised test results, a typical Standard 3 class (of children aged eight to ten) will contain children with reading ages ranging from seven to twelve years. Such variations present a challenge for the teacher, but they also provide interesting opportunities for pupils to learn from one another.

Middle school reading serves a variety of purposes. In junior school children often progress rapidly in reading just for the pleasure of mastering a new skill — many of them come to school with a strong desire to learn to read. How can we maintain the enthusiasm and freshness of five-year-olds? It helps if the middle school child can see the many faces of reading, can realise the rich variety of materials and the differing purposes for which we read. So at school we would encourage the middle school child to read the newspaper to find out what is happening in the local community, to consult reference books to seek out information for projects, to read novels for enjoyment, poetry for an expression of emotion... the list goes on. It is constrained only by the availability of materials and/or the combined imaginations of the teacher and child. Unless children realise that reading is a source of valuable knowledge about themselves and the culture in which they live they will never become truly literate adults. Unless they see that reading is functional, that it can help them achieve their ends, that it can produce answers to problems, and help entertain and amuse them, they will not become hooked on reading.

What aims do our teachers have in reading?

Over recent years a high degree of consensus has emerged amongst primary school teachers about the most desirable aims in teaching reading. While many teachers in other countries tend to espouse the view that children should be taught to decode with accuracy, to comprehend the author's message correctly, and that they should follow a prescribed set of graded readers until they master the basic skills, New Zealand teachers have charted a different course. Most reading instruction in New Zealand primary schools follows some form of 'natural language' or 'whole language' philosophy, which is essentially child-centred, driven by children's interests, with a dominant emphasis on gaining meaning from the outset.

According to several surveys (eg, Elley, 1985; Wagemaker, 1993) the aim of New Zealand teachers', first and foremost, is: 'to develop in children a lasting interest in reading', rather than 'to improve comprehension', 'extend vocabulary' or 'develop critical skills'. While such aims are not ignored in the classroom, the ideal which most teachers accept, is that children will develop these other desirable activities incidentally, if they read often a wide variety of materials, and discuss what they read with others. Much reading then is done in groups, where teacher and child share a good story, or where the teacher guides the group through a challenging text, using questions and discussion. A lasting interest in reading will more often follow, in this view, if teachers provide good role models, read to and with children, provide a rich source of interesting books, allocate time for silent reading, and encourage children to talk about the books they read. There is little emphasis then, on structured programmes, written comprehension exercises or formal tests. Rather, children are taught in a non-threatening, high-interest context, using a variety of methods and materials, all calculated to enhance interest. Reading sessions for most children are designed to be enjoyable sessions. Learning takes place but it is frequently incidental learning, occurring at the point of interest or need, rather than structured lessons with a mastery of a sequence of preordained skills and strategies.

The idea that much of children's learning takes place incidentally is well documented in the case of children's vocabulary acquisition. Several US studies have shown that children learn many new words from silent reading texts which are pitched at an appropriate level of difficulty (eg, Nagy et al, 1985). Miller and Gildea (1987) suggest that children learn up to 5000 words a year 'from conversational interactions supplemented by reading' (1987:88). These researchers argue that the sheer number of words able to be understood by children precludes direct, systematic teaching as an explanation for the range of children's vocabularies. Other experimental studies have shown that seven and eight year olds acquire many new words while listening to stories read aloud (Elley, 1989). Such findings are particularly important for slow or reluctant readers, who would not gain so much exposure to text by silent reading alone. Despite this encouraging research, it would be a mistake to assume that learning cannot be fostered by active intervention on the part of the teacher. Later sections of this chapter will elaborate on how teachers can enhance children's comprehension.

What materials are used in the middle school?

Middle school reading is characterised by texts that contain more difficult and more abstract concepts than those of the junior school. For example, *T Shirts* (discussed in the previous chapter) is an entertaining piece of writing which requires no more complex interpretation by the reader than the ability to recognise colour and repeat a similar syntactical pattern for each sentence on the page. Compare that with *My Dad Drinks* by David Hill which describes a boy's reactions to his birthday party that is spoilt by an alcoholic father who came home drunk. The latter story is multi-layered and a number of interpretations, some of them conflicting, can be held by the reader.

During the middle school years the term 'whole language approach' is seen at its best. This is a catch-all phrase which implies children and teachers working together towards developing literacy in all its forms, based on the children's interests and using books and stories that have literary quality and something to say. It implies that reading and writing activities are integrated with oral language, each feeding into the other. It can be contrasted with a formal approach based on graded readers and contrived worksheets, where the aims and exercises are similar for all, and where the materials and the teacher dictate the pace at which children work. Primary school teachers are not constrained, as they are at secondary school, by the demands of external examinations which so often prescribe what books shall be read. Most children are still keen

Group processes enhance comprehension.

to learn, eager to explore the world of knowledge, and to exercise the reading strategies they acquired during the first two years of school. The middle school classroom teacher, faced with a class of young readers, and a good supply of first rate books and School Journals has, in the authors' opinion, the most enjoyable teaching in the entire school system!

Learning Media (formerly School Publications), an arm of the Ministry of Education, is the chief provider of reading materials for middle school classrooms. Surveys have shown that 84 per cent of teachers use School Journals as the prime source of instructional reading material (Smith:45). The seventy-seven teachers in Henson's (1991) national survey reported overwhelmingly that School Journals were the most useful resource they used. Teachers described the journals to Henson as:

> *sensitive, relevant, current, varied, real stuff, a reflection of New Zealand society, colourful, easily handled, well illustrated, high interest, gender sensitive, multi-racial, able to cut through society's socio-economic barriers.(1991:17)*

Journals are produced at four levels:

	Number of issues annually	Target reading age
Part One	five	seven-eight
Part Two	four	eight-nine
Part Three	three	nine-eleven
Part Four	three	eleven-thirteen

In addition to these Journals a Junior Journal is produced annually. This is designed to fill a gap in materials for children who have finished the Ready to Read series but are not yet able to cope with Part One School Journals. From time to time a School Journal Story Library is produced when suitable material is available. The stories in this Library are characterised by high interest — low vocabulary, and are designed to appeal to older children who have difficulty with reading. In alternate years an extra journal of young peoples' writing has been produced. All Journals are issued free to schools in quantities based on the size of the school roll.

Each Journal contains a mixture of stories, plays, poems and non-fiction articles. Careful attempts are made to reflect the ethnic composition of society, both in the content of the writing and by encouraging writers who are not white and middle class. A recent analysis of ethnic representation in the Journals (Caddick, 1992) revealed that Maori characters typically made up about 10 per cent of those portrayed, Pacific Islanders 5 per cent and Asians 5 per cent. Part One and Two Journals have published cartoon strips in Maori and intend in future to publish some of the children's writing from bilingual schools. The editors of journals spend time in schools working with children and receive feedback from both teachers and students. As with Ready to Read, both children and teachers influence the content of the journals.

As well as School Journals, 86 per cent of middle school classes use trade books on a daily basis as part of the instructional programme. Books are obtained from the National Library Service, from school libraries and from specialist book publishers who sell paper back editions of quality children's books directly to children through the school.

Non-fiction is a genre needing special attention as it is read by only a few children. Fred and Jeanne Biddulph (1993) argue that there are two reasons why non-fiction is less popular with children. The first is that teachers set vague purposes for asking children to read non-fiction and secondly that most non-fiction is written by adults with an adult point of view and holds little interest for children. The Biddulphs' call for:

> Non-fiction that is based on children's ideas, experiences, questions and
> interests, as well as 'expert' views....This requires research with children and

> *teachers in classrooms to find out what the children are interested in, what ideas they hold about a topic, what they would like to find out, what language they use when they are discussing things in the world around them, what analogies they draw, and what connections they make to other things around them.(1993:16)*

School Journals do attempt to fill the gap in non-fiction writing but there is a constant need for teachers to seek out well written non-fiction books and encourage children to read them.

Books and Journals carry on with the teaching concepts established in the Ready to Read series. The emphasis is on the story and getting meaning. Journal articles are loosely graded for difficulty, with the aid of the Elley Noun Count formula (Elley and Croft, 1989). Other factors, such as interest, are also taken into account when considering the overall difficulty level of a story.

The appearance of the material is important. Compared with the large basal readers of American series, School Journals look like magazines, while the book component of the reading programme is carried out with real books written by established children's authors. No commercially produced worksheets are used. The result is a reading programme where the task of reading is carried out with a wide range of attractive everyday materials. Children do not have the added task of transferring the specific skills learnt from worksheets to real books, and the meaningful contexts of a story.

If they are to maintain and develop their interest in reading, children need to be given control in selecting the books they read. Halliday (1982) surveyed children's reading interests in Wellington. She reported that children tend to be indiscriminate readers of non-fiction. She also found that war books were popular, as well as books of jokes and riddles. She observed that there was an 'insatiable demand for books about dinosaurs'. In a survey of primary pupils in seventy-five Christchurch classrooms, Elley (1985) found an enormous range of favourite books and authors. Most popular at that time were Roald Dahl and Bill Peet (with boys and girls), Enid Blyton and Carolyn Keene (mostly girls), while Dr Suess and Margaret Mahy were often cited by younger pupils. Such a list differs considerably from a comparable survey conducted over a decade earlier (Elley and Tolley, 1972). Doubtless, another more recent survey would show differences again. As for children's favourite books, the 1985 survey showed a tremendous range. Very few were mentioned by more then three or four pupils. In the IEA Survey of 177 primary schools, it was found that 41 per cent of Standard 3 pupils reported reading books for pleasure in their own time nearly every day. Only 10 per cent read comics that often and 7 per cent read magazines at that age (Wagemaker, 1993).

Teachers need to be aware of the variety of children's reading material available — from books in comic form such as *Tin-tin* and *Asterix*, through popular authors such as Joy Cowley and Tessa Duder (as well as lesser known writers), to magazines dealing with popular music and sports heroes. Good reading teachers keep up with fashions in pupils' reading. Children may not continue as readers unless they have a measure of control in selecting the books they read, and an opportunity to compare notes on what they like. One wonders how often children are consulted about buying books for the school library.

How can we help children to improve their comprehension?

Conscious strategies to enhance children's comprehension are the hallmark of good middle school teaching. We consider comprehension to be an active process whereby a reader interacts with a text to produce meaning. The resultant meaning may or may not be similar to that intended by the author.

Comprehension is not something that usually happens unaided. It is not a plant that grows from the ground untended. It needs careful nurturing, occasional pruning and plenty of fertiliser if it is to flourish. In short, good teaching is necessary where children and teachers collaborate in generating meanings from texts.

Any pedagogy of comprehension needs to be grounded in valid theory and be practical in a classroom situation. Frank Smith's (1979) well-known maxim that 'you learn to read by reading' is only part of the picture. The teacher must foster the conditions that encourage children to learn to read by reading. If a child enters the middle school classes as a fluent reader it is easy to assume that the role of the teacher is to supply interesting books and leave the child to get on with it. On the contrary, the teacher still has a key pedagogical role to play.

Comprehension is a process concerned with large units of understanding and is not just the ability to answer questions from a text. Our obsession with comprehension exercises — usually answering questions — has fragmented teaching and ignored vital elements such as the purpose for which the reading was done. Not all reading is the same. If, for instance, I am looking up a telephone number for Zaggery I do not start at the A's and work through the book until I reach the Z's. My intended purpose is best served by a much more efficient strategy based on my knowledge of the structure of a telephone book. If, however, I am fascinated by the character of Manny Rat in *The Mouse and his Child* (Hoban, 1967) I will want to read every part of the story. Much of comprehension is determined by the purpose of the reading and too often the purposes for the reading have been to answer ten questions. Naturally children will develop strategies to cope — an obvious one is to read the questions first, read the story until a sentence is found with some of the same words as the question and then copy out the sentence. Usually such results are effective enough for the strategy to become a permanent part of a child's reading repertoire.

How then do we understand text? Rosenblatt (1985) has developed a promising theory of how it is done. Her work unites the psychological study of comprehension with traditions of literary criticism. Rosenblatt is a 'constructivist'. She claims that meaning lies not in the text, but is a creation of the readers as they bring all their relevant ideas, beliefs and feelings to the reading. This coming together of reader and text is a 'transaction' that affects both, and produces new, unique meanings.

Rosenblatt believes that it is important to distinguish between the reading process suited to poems, stories or plays, from that which characterises non-fiction. The process of reading plays, poems or stories is called *aesthetic reading* by Rosenblatt. By contrast, *efferent reading* occurs when the reader reads to acquire new information, such as a number in a phone book or how to make muffins from a recipe book. Aesthetic reading requires interpretations of a text on multiple levels — what happened, why did it happen, how did the participants feel? By contrast, a paraphrase by another reader can often serve for an efferent reading. Both aesthetic and efferent reading are necessary for literacy, and a competent reader will vary his/her stance according to purpose. Teaching and evaluation, however, often focus mainly on efferent styles of reading. Thus, it is possible to teach narrative texts in an efferent fashion, concentrating only on the surface features of the story, but if the aim of teaching comprehension strategies is to foster the habits of reading for pleasure throughout one's life, the aesthetic dimensions of stories must not be neglected.

Comprehension as a transaction

A transactional view of comprehension recognises that meaning does not lie solely with the printed word, nor does it rely solely on the world view the reader brings to the page. Meaning is a result of interaction between the print and the reader and, in a classroom situation, other readers who may be reading the same text. The reader is an active constructor of meaning — not an empty bucket to be filled with knowledge. Even texts which are read in ways Rosenblatt would call efferent are subject to this transactional process. For example, recipe books often give measurements in teaspoon quantities. Teaspoon measures vary in size according to whether the book is published in America or New Zealand. So the reader interprets them differently, according to their location.

Research in this tradition (Rosenblatt, 1983; Pressley and Gaskins, 1992;) has focused on transactional strategies which describe how comprehension can be fostered in the middle school. Amongst the more promising strategies studied are: activating prior knowledge; constructing images; summarising; predicting and checking predictions; trying to imagine how characters feel; thinking aloud; and self-questioning. Transactional strategies are learnt by:

> making students aware of the purposes of strategies, how and why they work and when and where they can be used. Students are given extensive practice in the context of ongoing school instruction, practice which produces a personalised mastery of the method. Students are actively involved in the evaluation, modification and construction of strategies. Teachers' do not give orders, but rather model, discuss, explain and re-explain, and in the process of doing so, teachers' understandings of strategies and their students change. Teachers and students are constructing new knowledge during strategy instruction. (Pressley et al, 1992)

Transactional strategies draw their theoretical underpinning from the work of Rosenblatt and are consistent with the views of Vygostsky and Bruner as described in Chapter 7. Chapter 2 contains a description of scaffolding used by Dacre with her preschooler, Polly. The principles are the same with middle school children, only the content is more demanding. As Pressley et al point out (1992), transactional teaching is also popular with whole language teachers (1992:529). However, it also allows for direct teaching and didactic explanation of what is happening. The classroom teacher has to recognise that an arsenal of strategies is required for assisting children in improving their comprehension. Which strategy to deploy will depend on the purpose of the reading, the material being read, the experiences of the children and whether the reading is done as a solitary activity or as part of a group.

> When reading as a group, the students and teacher act together, deciding when to apply particular strategies and when to advance, modify, or reject certain interpretations. The reading group process is thus highly strategic, using strategies appropriately and generating many alternative perspectives on material being read.(1992:513)

The teacher's role is to provide the readers with a range of appropriate strategies by modelling, discussion and direct instruction. As the reading progresses children may provide strategies for the group and suggest ways in which the story can be interpreted which have not occurred to the teacher. There is a continual interaction between teacher and reader where both may be modifying their strategy as the reading progresses through the text and sometimes modifying strategies in response to the text.

The long term aim of this approach is that children will use these strategies themselves when they read. Pressley et al describe the process as:

> Long participation in such a group is hypothesised to result in internalization of the 'executive' activities of the group. That is, the types of decisions once made by and in the group are eventually made by the individual participant when he or she reads alone.(1992:516)

Eeds and Wells (1989) have applied a transactional model to classroom teaching. They contrast a transactional view with the 'gentle inquisitions' of traditional comprehension teaching where the teacher poses questions and the children answer. Eeds and Wells consider that dialogue, where the group constructs and discloses deeper meanings, is a more appropriate way to develop understandings of text. Theoretical support for this approach is drawn from Vygotsky who maintained that the internal processes necessary for learning are only able to develop when children are interacting with people in their environment and in co-operation with their peers.

A relevant study carried out by Eeds and Wells used seventeen student teachers who met with a group of five to seven children twice a week for thirty minutes. Each group contained children with a range of reading ability. Student-teachers were used because it was felt that they would approach the task with few preconceived ideas as to what should happen in reading sessions. Eeds and Wells prepared the student-teachers in the following manner:

> We discouraged preparation of a set of explicit comprehension questions which reflected how they (the student-teachers) had read the text and advocated letting the meaning emerge in the group discussion, although we also stressed that they should be unafraid to seize a teachable moment if they recognised one. We wanted students and leaders to share their personal transactions with the text and go from there to what might emerge — dialogue or no.(1989:7)

In the course of this study, four studies were selected for in-depth analysis. Discussion sessions were transcribed and analysed. Four books were read by the children: *Tuck Everlasting* by Natalie Babbits, *After the Goat Man* by Betsy Byars, *Harriet the Spy* by Louise Fitzhugh and *The Dark Angel* by Meredith Pierce. An analysis of the transcriptions showed four major strategies emerging — *Constructing simple meaning, personal involvement, inquiry* and *critique*. These are elaborated below:

1   Constructing simple meaning involved discussion and recounting what happened in the story. Problems in understanding events described in the story were resolved. This is the sorting out stage in comprehension where basic concepts are clarified and an agreed upon meaning is sought.

2   Personal involvement was a recounting of personal stories inspired by the reading or discussion. Eeds and Wells comment that:

> being able to talk about the text in oblique or personal ways seemed to help students develop the personal significance the text had for them.... Sometimes the comments seemed irrelevant at the time but a close examination showed that they were important clues revealing how the students experiences were being linked up in the text.(1989:18)

3   During the inquiry phase, readers actively questioned what they were reading in an effort to construct meaning.

4   The critique occurred when the readers described what they liked and why they liked it. During this stage of discussion:

> just about all elements of literary criticism emerged. While the children may not have known the technical names for them, the development of character, plot, language, time place, mood, and theme emerged naturally as part of group talk.(1989:23)

Although Eeds and Wells reported part of their study (tallying the children's comments according to categories) as quantifiable data, they considered the overall outcomes of the process to be more important than a simple categorisation of comments. Children in the groups:

> recalled, they verified recall, they inferred, they supported their inferences they read critically — evaluating the text and their understanding of it, and discussing with insight and clarity how it was that the author 'did it to them'. Each group became collaborative rather than competitive. Atmospheres were

created which encouraged such risk taking behaviours as Ben's who admitted in his group that 'he always cries at the end'.(1989:26)

This description is typical of the kind of classroom dialogue which occurs in many of the best New Zealand middle school classes, as teachers use guided reading lessons to model and extend the comprehension process. Clearly it requires sensitive teachers who are willing to give up their role as arbiter of what the story is about.

Reciprocal teaching

A more structured approach to helping children learn useful comprehension strategies is found in the work pioneered by American researchers Palinscar and Brown (1984), but is now finding a place in many New Zealand classes. This approach is referred to as *Reciprocal Teaching*. It requires small group teaching in which the teacher models various reading strategies and then the children take over the teacher's role and follow suit.

The four strategies involved in this approach are:

1   Clarifying — where the focus of attention is directed towards understanding the author's message in a chosen segment of the text.

2   Questioning — which is used to encourage children to formulate questions against which their own understandings of the text can be clarified.

3   Summarising — which helps the reader separate relevant information from unimportant details and also assists the reader in organising information from consecutive paragraphs.

4   Predicting — where the reader attempts to use all available knowledge to make a prediction of what might follow next.

Reciprocal teaching shares with the approach of Eeds and Wells the ultimate aim of empowering the reader with the strategies which will allow an independent reading of the text without the intervention or authority of an adult reader acting as referee. It has as a foundation the belief that meaning has to be actively constructed by the reader following the processes outlined above. The approach is more structured than that of Eeds and Wells who place the teacher as a member of the group whose interpretation is of no more or less value than any other group member.

Gilroy and Moore (1988) used reciprocal comprehension fostering activities to improve the comprehension skills of twenty-eight girls drawn from Standard 3 to Form 2 in Auckland schools. The subjects were selected because their comprehension scores were two years below their chronological age. The procedures developed by Palinscar and Brown were taught to the girls for twenty-one days. That is, they were taught, and given time to practise, the skills of summarising, questioning, clarifying and predicting. Teaching consisted of modelling the four appropriate strategies to be adopted. Then the subjects in turn modelled the behaviour and taught other members of the group. The progress of the experimental group was compared with the progress made by two control groups, one of average comprehenders and one of above average comprehenders.

The results were impressive. The baseline comprehension score for the experimental group was approximately half the level of both control groups. By the end of the intervention, all experimental groups had achieved at a level equal to, or greater than, the average control group and close to the above average control group. What is even more interesting about these findings is that a follow-up survey carried out eight weeks after the intervention had finished, showed that the experimental groups had continued to improve. Gains the subjects made were soundly based and durable — the subjects continued to improve during the follow-up phase of the study.

Another study, conducted in Auckland by Kelly and Moore (1993), showed that two experimental groups made an average gain of 20 percentage points during the experimental phase, while a control group showed no equivalent gains. Kelly and Moore describe the daily format of instruction as follows:

> *Each day the teachers started with a discussion, everyone trying to predict the content from the title. Following silent reading each child then took a turn at (1) devising a 'teacher-like' question, (2) thinking of a short summary, (3) predicting what would happen next in the passage, and if necessary, (4) seeking clarification of some point. During the early sessions the teachers modelled the strategies extensively but with practice the students became more adept, so the teachers were able to reduce their scaffold or support and act more as a coach in providing corrective feedback and praise.(1993:2)*

Reciprocal teaching of comprehension is an effective teaching strategy because it directly addresses metacognition — how we learn. By modelling and showing exactly how a reader makes summaries, formulates questions, clarifies what has happened in the text and predicts what may happen next, a fluent reader can assist a less fluent reader to bring meaning to the printed page. The less fluent reader models the technique and increases his/her own skills. Gilroy and Moore found that their subjects could use the techniques effectively not only during the study but also elsewhere, for reading in a variety of materials, covering a range of subject areas. American research on reciprocal teaching confirms that this makes a substantial contribution to improved comprehension with upper primary school children and beyond.

Individualised instruction

While much comprehension teaching is carried out in groups, some programmes are designed for individual children. Holdaway (1972) was one of the first to develop an individualised programme for New Zealand and elements of his method are still widely adopted. It is described as: 'a pattern of classroom organization within which different patterns of teaching may be used depending on the needs of different children and the style of the particular teacher.'(1972:40) The principles upon which the programme is based are described as 'self-selection, self-seeking, self-pacing, self-evaluation and self-sharing.' (1972:40-41) The children select their own materials from a wide range available in the class, determine their own goals for the reading, read at their own pace, evaluate their own progress and share what they have learnt from their reading with others. The role of the teacher is to provide a wide range of materials based on knowledge of the children, to motivate the class and to conference regularly with individuals and groups of children.

At the heart of this method is the individual conference with the teacher. Holdaway describes the conference as:

> one of the most satisfying aspects of the programme but it also tends to present the greatest difficulties. The teacher schedules to interview five or six children every day. This means spending no more than four to six minutes with each child, and most teachers find it very difficult to limit themselves in this way.(1972:55)

During the conference the teacher's role is to establish rapport, to share with the child insights about the reading, to question, to record progress, and to provide encouragement and guidance.

In the twenty years since Holdaway set out his structure for individualising reading we have developed our knowledge of the way meaning is constructed by the reader as a result of interactions with the text, as well as developing a theoretical basis for our understanding of the way group processes develop meanings from text. Nevertheless, there is clearly an important role for an individualised approach at times. Contrary to some opinion, Holdaway is at pains to point out that individualised reading does not preclude group work, when he claims that, 'major teaching and practice must still be organized on a group basis.' (1972:56)

Holdaway has had an important influence because he drew to the attention of teachers the importance of self in reading — self selection, self pacing and self evaluation.

Conclusion

This chapter has outlined some of the most promising trends in reading practice in the middle school. In addition to the basic core of methods used at all levels — shared reading, guided reading and independent reading — teachers in the middle school have found ways to enhance their children's comprehension, and their love of books, by conducting real 'transactional' dialogues about the books they share; by promoting such active strategies as clarifying, summarising, questioning and predicting, and by allowing for individualised instruction, with conferences.

There is much more to the teaching of comprehension, and the topic is taken up again in secondary reading, using schema theory as a base. In addition, we should draw attention to other promising leads in the research.

For instance, Long, Winograd and Bridge (1989) showed the importance of helping children create mental imagery in their reading; Pickens and McNaughton (1988) described how peer tutoring can improve comprehension and this is now common practice in many schools; Stein and Glenn (1979) showed the potential of helping children understand story grammar, or the way stories are structured; Wittrock's (1975) research has revealed the benefits of helping children actively generate associations as they read. All of this research is contributing to a greater understanding of reading comprehension, but no one concept contains the answer to providing children with appropriate strategies. As always, teachers need to tailor their methods to suit their children's needs.

Chapter 6

Reading in the secondary school

Secondary school lasts for approximately five years for most children — from age thirteen when the child leaves primary or intermediate school to seventeen when children complete the seventh form. Sixteen is the legal age for leaving school in New Zealand but because of the difficulty of finding work, most students stay at school until they have completed the sixth form. An increasing number are remaining to Form 7.

Secondary schools are organised differently from primary and intermediate schools. Teaching is more specialised with different teachers for each subject area. Nicholson (1985:518) has described high school teaching as lecturing rather than teaching, although many teachers today would find that judgement a harsh one. The day is divided into periods (usually five a day) and students change rooms for each period. 'Reading' as a subject does not normally appear on the timetable. 'English' is a compulsory subject for all students in the first three years of secondary school and includes a number of set books to be read, most of which are novels. Reading instruction is usually seen as remedial rather then developmental, and most secondary schools employ a reading teacher to work with the weaker or reluctant readers. Such teachers are usually ex-primary teachers, and many work on a part-time basis. The phrase 'Reading across the Curriculum' is much bandied about in secondary schools. This notion is designed to promote the idea that reading is important in all secondary subjects eg, English, Science, Social Studies, Mathematics, Accounting, Foreign Languages; and that every teacher is a teacher of reading and writing. In reality, however, the bulk of the reading teaching which does occur is still undertaken by the reading or English teacher.

External examinations cast a cold shadow over the secondary school curriculum, particularly in the senior levels of the school. In his analysis of secondary students' literature results in the IEA study, Purves (1979) warned of the stultifying hand of examination syllabii. He wrote:

> Achievement in literature in New Zealand secondary schools means not only reading a text with clear comprehension but mastering an academic approach to what one reads. Some hints exist that these kinds of learning accompany a lessened interest in and involvement with literature. One may well ask whether such a state of affairs is desirable, particularly given the fact that relatively few students who take English in Forms Six and Seven actually go on to be

scholars in literature or professional critics....One must wonder about the appropriateness of the examinations to the lives of the students.(1979:67)

Despite some examination reform, and greater use of internal assessment for school leaving certificates, Purves' comments are still relevant today. While School Certificate may be changing and diminishing in importance, the seventh form University Bursary examinations in English still determines what senior school students will read officially. Only a minority of secondary students go on to some form of English study at tertiary level and the 'academic' nature of the seventh form prescriptions, driven as they are by university requirements is designed for the few. As the employment situation in New Zealand continues to worsen for young people, and more students stay at school until they are seventeen or eighteen, the reading which secondary students are expected to do will have to reflect to a greater extent the interests and aspirations of a majority of students who have no interest in academic study.

Teaching

Tom Nicholson (1984) has conducted the most intensive New Zealand research into reading in the secondary school. Nicholson had four research questions:

1   What kinds of reading tasks are assigned to students in the junior secondary schools in the subject areas of Science, English, Mathematics and Social Studies?

2   What kinds of knowledge are required for students to be able to complete the reading tasks assigned to them?

3   What kinds of strategies do students use in order to cope with these reading tasks?

4   What strategies are used by low progress readers in order to complete these tasks?

The researchers spent six months in two classrooms with a third and fourth form. By using a concurrent interview technique, that is, by questioning and talking with the students during the course of their lessons a picture was obtained of what the students were actually doing as opposed to what their teachers thought they were doing.

Reading tasks were different depending upon the subject area. In English, for example, students were expected to read and comment upon poems, novels and plays, complete worksheets on spelling and write essays. In Science students were expected to conduct experiments, interpreting and writing up the results. They were required to consult their science text books which frequently used graphs and tables. Social Studies required library research and often reading maps, interpreting bar graphs and tables.

Knowledge of the way the texts operated was necessary for successful reading in the classes Nicholson observed. Difficulties with the text were either a result of inappropriate ideas held by the reader or a result of a text itself which was difficult to understand because of specialised vocabulary, poor layout or confused diagrams. 'Reader based confusions were often due to mismatch between students' everyday knowledge of terms such as 'range' or 'markets' and the special meaning of those terms in say maths and social studies.' (1984:440) One student for example thought the term 'stockbroker' referred to a shepherd.

Students used a variety of strategies to complete the reading tasks. For instance, one student read the question then looked for similar words in the passage. When she found them she copied them out. Often this provided the correct answer — and if so, it was probably a poor question.

The results of this study showed that there was frequently a large gap between the teachers' perceptions of what the students were understanding from the task, and what the students were actually understanding. Reading tasks varied widely across the subject areas. Students did not understand the specialised vocabulary used in particular subjects nor did they understand the syntax of the material. Diagrams were not explained and the teachers were mistaken in their assumptions that the students had sufficient background knowledge to understand what they were meant to be reading. In Nicholson's words:

> The surface structure of the classroom can suggest to the teacher that the content is being learned, while in the minds of the students there is only a maze of confusion. It seems obvious and banal to conclude that teachers ought to spend more time talking with their pupils. (1984:450-459)

Improving reading comprehension

How can secondary students be taught to improve their reading comprehension? It is easy to criticise the current scene in secondary reading, but we need to suggest improvements. Can we do better? Research from several overseas countries — Durkin (1976) in the United States; Morris (1986) in Australia; Lunzer and Gardner (1979) in the UK — indicates that most teachers do very little to help their students improve their comprehension. In an observational survey of thirty-nine US classrooms, across fourteen school systems (Durkin, 1978), only forty-five minutes (out of 18 000 minutes of observation) was used in teaching comprehension. Apparently most teachers are unaware of what can be done to help. Comparable figures are lacking for the New Zealand scene, but there is surely room for more productive time on this topic.

In recent years, more and more attention has been devoted to research on improving comprehension. Pearson and Fielding (1991) in the United States and Cairney (1990) in Australia have effectively summarised the findings and implications of this research. Much of it has been conducted within a tradition of *schema theory*.

Study skills are a key element in secondary reading.

What is schema theory?

One psychological explanation of how meaning-making occurs, and how knowledge is stored and organised in the brain, is called schema theory. Briefly, schema refers to the frameworks of knowledge we store in our brains to represent familiar things and ideas in our experience. A schema is an abstract mental structure, containing the generalised characteristics of the object in question. Thus we have a schema for cars, another for houses, for books, for justice. Such schema are built up as a result of repeated experience with these things, and so every person's schema is unique. Keen fishermen have elaborate schema for fish; fashion designers for clothes.

When a reader (or listener) encounters a new example of a thing for which they have a schema, they can slot it into the appropriate place, and locate it more readily then if no such schema existed. When John, a car enthusiast, reads about the virtues of a new red Porsche in a car magazine, he readily integrates them into his elaborate schema for cars, and will probably recall them efficiently. However, the description of the reasons for the national trade imbalance which restricted the import of such cars may not be slotted in if John has no relevant schema for such economic concepts.

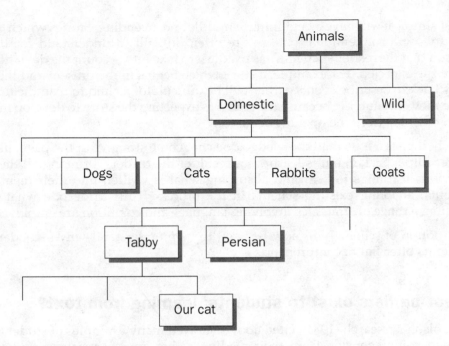

Figure 1 Possible schema for animals

Our schema are infinitely divisible into smaller categories. I have a schema for animals which may be divided into large/small animals or domestic animals and wild animals (see Figure 1 above). Under domestic schema we may have schema for cats, dogs, rabbits or goats. We can continue these subdivisions until our own family cat occupies his or her own particular niche. Such an organisation of mental structures enables us quickly to 'slot into place' incoming information from a text or a conversation.

Schema making rarely occurs at the conscious level, except perhaps where completely new knowledge is to be acquired. New things, be they ways to change the tyre on a car, or details of the settlement of New Zealand, are most efficiently learnt when they can be attached to preexisting schema. In the process, both the pre-existing and the new knowledge may be slightly changed. Schema provide an efficient way of organising our knowledge of the world. As human beings we know a vast number of things — about every aspect of life. To make sense of this huge amount of information we acquire, just by virtue of being alive, we must organise it in some way, because our capacity to remember discrete amounts of information is limited. With the benefit of elaborate, well organised schema, relevant to the text they read, children can predict better what is to come, fill in the gaps in the author's account, recall better what is read, and even stand back and evaluate it more effectively.

As well as having schema which will accommodate the content of the story, readers also have a schema for the story itself. That is, they will expect something to happen in the story and that it will be organised in a particular way. At its most simple it will have a beginning, a middle and an ending. Stories which do not follow a conventional pattern are often difficult to understand for the reason that the reader's schema has to adjust to take into account the deviation from the expected. For example, a story which begins in the present and then goes back to describe events earlier will be difficult for a child to read the first time they encounter it, because the reader is expecting the story to develop in a linear fashion from the opening sentence.

Psychologists tell us that knowledge does not come straight off the page, like water into a bucket, but is learnt as a result of the readers' bringing all their previous learnings to bear and absorbing what is written into their mental schema, adapting existing schema in the process. Thus to decode what is written, a range of strategies involving language and cognition are employed.

The notion of schema will now be used to help understand why secondary students often fail to comprehend.

What barriers exist to students' learning from text?

Nicholson's research (1984), cited above, showed many examples of students' limited comprehension from their reading. Other lines of research confirm these problems. In a large survey of third form student's comprehension of their prescribed textbooks, Elley (1975) showed that well over half were unable to understand their texts well enough to learn from them. In a comparable study of Polytechnic apprentices learning from hand-outs in a variety of courses, Marriott and Elley (1984) showed very similar findings. Many students are asked to read material for which they are ill-equipped. What are the major barriers? How can we help them overcome such barriers? Schema theory provides one useful way to conceptualise these problems.

Barriers to reading comprehension

1 **Lack of relevant schema.** If students are asked to read material for which they have no related schema, no relevant background knowledge, they will neither understand it, nor recall it. Too often, textbook writers assume that the readers have experience which they do not have. Too often, they believe that just by mentioning a novel concept once, students will grasp it, full-blown, and be able to think with it as efficiently as one who has had regular exposure to it. Defining a concept is not enough. New concepts are notoriously slow to develop, especially if they are abstract, and defined without examples. Visual images, familiar analogies, concrete illustrations and class discussion will help connect the new concept to familiar ones. Repeated exposure in motivating circumstances will also assist. Thus, a Form 4 mathematics text informs students that 'a *relation* is a set of ordered pairs. The first *element* of each ordered pair is usually connected to the second by a rule. The *domain* is the set of first elements of the ordered pairs. The *range* is the set of second elements of the ordered pairs.'

For the writer, such terms may be clear and obvious. For the uninitiated, however, they are meaningless. They would be quite unhelpful, without many examples and practical experiences which promote their use, and help establish appropriate schema for the student. Much prose in mathematics and science texts is precise exposition, with little room for variation in reader interpretation.

Recognising the importance of background schema, it is clear that the English teacher cannot solve the reading problems of the Mathematics or Science teacher. Schema building is every teacher's responsibility. Teaching better decoding skills, or prediction skills, or self-correction strategies is irrelevant here. Before a class is asked to read complex expository material containing unfamiliar concepts, it is important to prime the students with prior discussion, visual aids, parallel concepts or related anecdote — any strategy to help establish relevant schema. In novels and plays, the context provides multiple helpful cues. For abstract mathematical texts, like the example above, this is not a solution.

2   **Lack of vocabulary — the labels for the schema**. Sometimes the writer, in an effort to impress, uses long, technical or obtuse terms. Students may have the relevant schema, but fail to recognise the author's language — the labels for the schema. All third formers have a schema for *spade*, but few would link it with a *manual excavation implement*. In the Polytechnic study mentioned above (Marriott and Elley, 1984), students often lost comprehension for this reason. A text question asked them to 'describe the operation of x'. For many this was unhelpful. When translated into 'how does x work?' there was no problem. And in a Christchurch study of fifth formers (Elley, 1983), difficult prose with unfamiliar vocabulary was read with comparative ease by students when the low frequency words (municipality, site, hamlet) were replaced with high frequency terms for the same schema (town, place, village). 'Considerate text' is user-friendly. It prefers the familiar to the unfamiliar term; it provides examples and analogies; it uses visual aids. When teachers realise that the text is inconsiderate, then comprehension instruction is called for.

3   **Failure to use relevant schema**. Sometimes barriers to comprehension occur because students do not see links between what they read and what they know. The key schema are not accessed as required. They are not properly prepared for arousing the schema. In earlier chapters, this problem has been addressed by recommending prior discussion, showing pictures, predicting events, imagining outcomes. For secondary school texts a similar principle applies. Students can be assisted to raise the relevant schema to consciousness, to readily accessible positions, by prior discussion, skimming the chapter, studying visuals, examining subheads — anything to rouse as many relevant thoughts and feelings as possible. Once the schema are primed, they are easy to call to the surface as required. Comprehension will be easier.

If the topic of the reading is natural disasters, prior class discussion will call forth many personal instances; if the topic is the South East Asian economy, the teacher may ask who has been to Singapore, or who knows someone from Malaysia. Television programmes, films, overseas visitors, wall pictures, are often helpful as prompts to pertinent schema. All such strategies are assisting children to improve their comprehension — in a wider range of contexts.

4   **Interference from inappropriate schema**. English words frequently have multiple meanings. The author has one meaning in mind, the reader conjures up another. In a chapter on government, a student reads that 'the Prime Minister sets up a *Cabinet*, and its members are called to the *House*'. It is easy to visualise how pupils might encounter interference from association with furniture rather then politics. How confusing it could be for students reading about the difference between *gasses* and *liquids*, when they recall that petrol is also called gas. The word *capital* has different meanings in economics, geography and social intercourse. A *metal* road is not made of metal; a local *market*, selling crafts or fruit, is different from the overseas markets sought by our exporters.

Nicholson's research (1984) cited above provides many such examples of interfering schema. Sensitive teachers are alert to potential confusions, or they provide opportunities, in discussion, for such misconceptions to emerge. Recognition of interference is a starting point for teaching comprehension.

5   **Unfamiliarity with common text schema**. Textbooks in different school subjects have different typical structures. Regular reading of narrative text sets up a schema for the normal structure of a good story — *setting, plot, problem, solution*. Children who read many stories learn these typical structures, often subconsciously. When they read another story, their story schema sets up expectations for the events of the story. They make better predictions, slot the story elements into their appropriate places, and recall them more readily (Stein and Glenn, 1979). Without such schema, the pattern is missing, the story is a jumbled maze.

Likewise there are characteristic text structures for scientific prose, for history, for mathematics. Some prose is organised in simple lists. *List structures* regularly include such signal words as 'first', 'second', 'to begin with'. These signal to the reader that the prose should be read as if it were a list of items in a sequential order. *Contrast* structures frequently contain such terms as 'however', 'but', 'on the one hand', 'on the other hand', 'while', 'yet', 'nevertheless', 'although', 'either-or', 'by contrast', etc. Some state a cause, then an effect. *Cause-and-effect structures* can be recognised by such cues as 'because', 'since', 'therefore', 'consequently', 'as a result', 'this led to', 'accordingly', 'thus', 'if-then'. Some structures provide a definition, followed by examples; some provide a theme, and then set up a contrast.

Examples of the differing structures are given in Figure 3 on page 65. A reading teacher will help her students by alerting them to these structures, identifying them when they are encountered in shared reading. Indeed, a discussion of the *signal words* which help students recognise the structure

1   List

2   Contrast - Comparison

3   Cause - Effect

4   Elaboration: Main point and examples

5   Top - Down Hierarchy

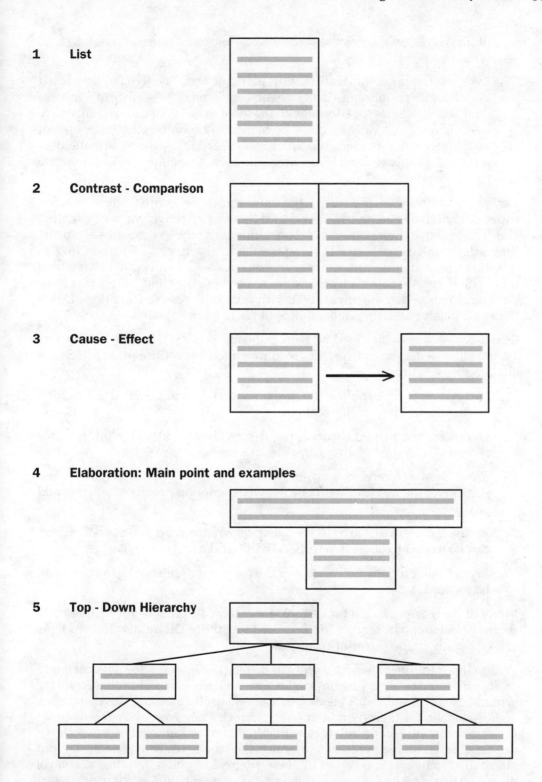

Figure 2 Common text structures

of a passage will assist them to predict, appreciate, integrate and recall what they read.

6   **Lack of strategies for dealing with difficult text**. The five barriers listed above relate to missing or inaccessible schema. The sixth problem is a dearth of strategies for coping with these barriers. What can students do to help themselves? How can they be helped to become better independent problem-solving readers of difficult text? Some teachers, impatient to move on, simply tell and hope. But telling is not teaching. New schema do not develop so easily.

Earlier chapters have identified the importance of guided silent reading transactional dialogue and reciprocal teaching as effective ways of assisting children improve their comprehension. Underlying these strategies is a belief that pupils will read better if they are reading actively — responding to questions, to predicting consequences, to summarising main points, to retelling favourite parts. Anything a teacher does to promote the child's view that he or she should approach a difficult text with active aggressive intentions rather than as a passive absorber of content is likely to be productive.

One useful system, which has had wide publicity, is the *SQ3R* model (Robinson, 1970). These letters stand for five recommended procedures when facing a challenging reading task:

1   *Survey*: Allow time to skim the chapter or text, looking at visuals, checking subheads, seeking main points.

2   *Question*: Ask probing questions to provide an authentic purpose for reading. Turn the headings into questions.

3   *Read*: Read actively to answer the questions set. Make links between sections of the text and with one's own experience; predict, challenge and criticise.

4   *Recite*: Self-test regularly to see whether what is read is understood and can be recited to oneself, or others, without the text.

5   *Review*: After a pause go back over the main points, ensuring that they can be recalled.

Many of the recommended procedures for better comprehension addressed in recent research can be readily incorporated into the SQ3R model, and students can be readily trained to adopt and practise it.

Within this tradition of active reading, Johnson (1990) conducted a recent study of fourth formers' learning in an English unit in Christchurch secondary schools. Two average ability classes were taught useful metacognitive strategies — how to monitor their own learning from text. They were shown how to set their goals, ask questions, relate new material to prior knowledge, break down the task into realistic sub-tasks, monitor their own comprehension, try out alternative strategies and reflect on their progress in understanding. A control group of two matched classes, which were not given such guidance, learned significantly less about the contents of the unit taught. While more such research is needed, there is clear support here for helping students improve their reading strategies with conscious, deliberate teaching. The bulk of evidence shows that comprehension can be promoted with teacher guidance. Comprehension can be taught (Dole et al, 1991; Haller et al, 1988).

Table 1 on page 68 analyses the core secondary school subjects along four dimensions — organisation, strategies, purposes and language. We suggest that by careful teaching, high school students can be made aware of these factors and thus improve their comprehension across all subject areas.

Access to materials

It is important that all secondary students have access to books at home and to a well-stocked library with up-to-date resources. What evidence do we have on this matter?

Lamb (1987) surveyed children at Form 2 and Form 5 to see how much written material children had access to in their homes. The study drew on a random stratified national sample of 2538 students at the Form 2 level and 2260 Form 5 students. The majority of students (74 per cent of Form 2 and 81 per cent of Form 5) had fifty or more books at home. In a parallel question in the 1990 survey of reading-literacy (Wagemaker, 1993), these figures were almost identical for Standard 3 and Form 4 children. Indeed, in this survey, 39 per cent claimed to have more then 200 books at home, at both age levels. Approximately 90 per cent of students in these surveys had access to a daily newspaper. As for access in the schools, a relatively bright picture of reading resources was painted in the same survey. (Wagemaker, 1993) Most students had ready access to books not only at home, but also in the local community libraries. At school, most classes had well-stocked classroom libraries, and New Zealand school libraries were amongst the largest in the survey. The average primary school library had over 4000 titles, rising to 17 500 in one case. None had less than 500. At secondary level, the average library contained nearly 10 000 books, and some had as many as 30 000. Not surprisingly, the schools with the largest libraries also showed the highest achievement levels — nationally and internationally. An adequate supply of books is an essential condition for a successful reading programme but it is not enough.

Unfortunately, not all students have equal access to resources. In the 1990 survey, the schools with large numbers of low-achieving readers tended to have pupils from homes with fewer books, and this divergent situation may well be deteriorating. Thus, a survey carried out in Canterbury secondary schools by Ashby (1986) showed a wide fluctuation in the amount of money spent on the school library. For example, a private boys school spent $12.50 per student on its library (the highest in the survey) followed by a private girls school ($11.43 per student) with the third highest outlay ($10) spent by a private boys school. By contrast the lowest expenditure ($2.14) was a state secondary girls school, the next lowest expenditure was also a state secondary

	Reader's purpose	Typical language	Typical organisation	Useful strategies
Science	Follow instructions Understand concepts Remember main points Report observations Deduce generalisations	Formal prose Technical terms Impersonal Abstractions, laws Every word important	Structured - subheadings - experiments Pictures, tables Main idea, then details	Survey chapter Note visuals Read carefully Relate to experience Check understanding Memorise main points

English literature	Enjoyment
	Interpret character
	Appreciate style
	Analyse plot
	Critically evaluate
		Personal, informal
		Diverse vocabulary
		Dialogue
		Expressive, emotive
		Action, humour, style
			Narrative style
			Story grammars - Setting
			      - Plot
			      - Climax
			      - Resolution
				Read quickly
				Follow story line
				Study character
				Predict outcomes
				Use context
				Critically evaluate

Mathematics	Learn concepts
	See patterns
	Understand number relations
	Solve problems
		Formal prose
		Precise definitions
		Quantities, symbols
		Abstractions
		Every word important
			Logical development
			Explanation
			      - Examples
			      - Exercises
				Read carefully
				Study model
				Interpret problems
				Transfer symbols exactly
				Check solutions
				Look for patterns

Social Studies	Identify main points Determine trends Consider implications Identify viewpoints Critically evaluate Interpret visuals	Formal prose Descriptive Technical terms Many visual aids	Structured - sub-headings - case-studies Maps, charts, pictures Main idea, then details (or vice-versa) Chronological sequence Causes - events - effects	Skim read for overview Study visuals, summaries Identify main points, trends Relate to own experience Contrast viewpoints

Table 1 Reading tasks across the curriculum

girls school ($2.67) while the third lowest ($2.87) was a state co-educational school.

Ashby comments that 'library budgets continue to fall behind inflation and the funding of school libraries is of major concern'. Decentralisation of school control has no doubt contributed to this variation between schools' resources.

What do we know about adolescents' reading habits?

A major purpose of teaching reading is to create regular reading habits. How successful are our schools in achieving this goal? The median time spent on reading for pleasure in Lamb's survey was four hours a week in the Form 2 group and three hours in the Form 5 group. What is disconcerting is that a quarter of the Form 5 group and nearly half of the Form 5 group reported that they disliked reading. Thus, although most New Zealand children have ready access to reading materials, not everyone has developed a lasting interest in reading as a result of their primary school programme.

To explore this matter in greater depth, we should examine the finding of several smaller studies. A survey of the sixth form girls at Wellington East Girls College was carried out in 1981, 1982 and 1983 by Janet Maconie. Within this school population are a diverse number of ethnic groups and the respondents included Chinese, Greek, Indian, Maori, Pacific Islanders and European girls. However, the majority of slow and reluctant readers would not have remained at school for the sixth form.

Reading was high on the list of preferred spare time activities, with 17 per cent of the girls placing it at the top of their preferred activities. Television, by contrast, was the preferred spare time activity for only 14 per cent. Nearly all the girls claimed to enjoy reading — only 8 per cent did not. These results conflict with Lamb's findings, but perhaps the subjects in this study enjoyed reading because they were more academically successful. They were the students who survived to the sixth form. Moreover, all surveys of reading habits show that girls read more often than boys.

A varied and interesting range of reading material was included. A majority read books rather than comics or magazines. Subject matter included present day love stories, historical novels, science fiction, stories about teenage relationships, mysteries, thrillers and religious books. The author comments that 'Maori and Samoan/Pacific Island interest in books with a discrimination theme was very noticeable and they were more interested in books about their own country and race.' (1984:3)

The final part of the survey asked the girls to name the five books they would choose if they could be had free. School texts do appear in this wish list but the most commonly chosen books were a trilogy from the best selling author Virginia Andrews. *Flowers in the Attic, If There be Thorns* and *Petals in the Wind* were the most popular choices. Maconie deplores this choice of author and finds it hard to accept that the peer group is a more influential factor in determining the reading habits of this group of teenagers than formal English teaching with its emphasis on 'quality' books.

The most recent and extensive study of secondary school reading habits was carried out by Bardsley (1991) who studied the reading habits of 2202 fourth and sixth formers from ten secondary schools in the Manawatu region. This is a more representative group, and did include both genders. From her survey she concluded that 19.3 per cent of respondents would be classified as 'ludic' readers, who reported that they enjoyed reading and read more than three to four books in one month, and were reading a non-school book at the time of the survey. 'Moderate' readers comprised 59 per cent of the sample. Moderate readers said they enjoyed reading and were reading at least one to two books a month. Reluctant readers (22 per cent of the sample) did not enjoy reading. They are the group most likely to read no books in a month. They also did most of their reading at school 'possibly only when compelled to read' Bardsley comments (1991:23). It is not possible to know what proportion of students could not read fluently in this group. However, it is important to note that of the total sample only twenty-eight (1.3 per cent) claimed that difficulty with reading was a reason for not enjoying reading.

When asked to rank books, magazines, comics and newspapers in order of popularity, reluctant and moderate readers in both the fourth and sixth form ranked magazines first. Comics were ranked second in popularity by reluctant readers in the fourth form and third in popularity by all other groups. Books were ranked first by ludic readers in the fourth and sixth form and by moderate readers in the fourth and sixth form (girls only) group. Also of note is the relative unpopularity of newspapers by ludic readers in the sixth form — they were ranked only fourth out of four choices.

Bardsley asked students to name the best book they had read recently. A quarter of the sample could not name any book. Seventeen per cent named books that were part of class sets. Of the 768 titles, 133 were from school class sets. Titles from the Sweet Valley High series were cited by 6 per cent of the sample and accounted for 192 titles. Nearly 20 per cent (153) were non-fiction titles, covering an extremely wide range of subjects.

When asked to name a favourite author Roald Dahl was cited most often particularly by fourth formers. Dahl was cited as a favourite author by 245 high school students from a total of 1513 who answered this item on the questionnaire. He was equally popular in a primary school survey in Christchurch (Elley, 1985). Second choice was Virginia Andrews, author of numerous horror books.(See Maconie's study, above.) Popular reading preferences at this age have not changed a great deal during the last decade. Interestingly, a New Zealand author, Margaret Mahy, was cited as the second most popular author among reluctant readers.

Bardsley has produced the most comprehensive and detailed study on teenagers and their reading in New Zealand. Within the fourth and sixth forms it is possible to identify distinct groups with similar reading habits. Maori and

Pacific Island boys are dependent on school for most of their reading. We also learn that for a quarter of the sample, school is the only place where they read at all. Among her recommendations Bardsley suggested that:

> *A recommended policy for teachers of English is to begin each English class*
> *with ten minutes of sustained silent reading. Students have the responsibility*
> *and established habit of carrying their own reading material with them. There*
> *is also a need to provide students with time just to browse, choose and read in a*
> *recreational sense.(1991:124)*

The total range of material read is vast and the question still needs to be asked whether teachers and school libraries adequately cater for the variety of students' reading interests.

Chapter 7

How do children read?
Some theoretical considerations

This section attempts to describe some of the theory which underpins our practices in New Zealand classrooms. To understand how we learn to read we have to understand many of the concepts describing human learning and development.

The importance of theory

A coherent and articulated theory of reading is necessary for all teachers. Whether we care to admit it or not, every action we take is governed or influenced in some way by our theories, large or small, comprehensive or specific. The act of writing this book is based on the simple theory that people who read books on such topics may be influenced by what they have read. When teachers praise children for virtuous actions, the teachers are applying a theory that praise is reinforcing and that such reinforcement will lead to a repetition of these actions. This is, in fact, part of a larger behavioural theory about ways of influencing people's conduct.

Teachers need to make their theories explicit and able to be communicated to other people. Hence a need for a clearly developed theory of reading which is articulated and can be understood by parents, children, review officers, Ministry officials, journalists, politicians and their advisers. It is not sufficient to argue that successful teaching has always been done in a particular way. If our theory is not articulated we are always vulnerable to groups or individuals who have a clearly expressed philosophy and expect teaching to be governed by their philosophy. Unless the teacher can provide a plausible counter view, the person with the clearly expressed philosophy will carry the day. As professionals, teachers must be prepared to argue logically against those who would reduce the teaching of reading to, for instance, a series of systematic phonics exercises, or the routine completion of worksheet exercises that accompany basal readers.

The philosophy underpinning much reading instruction in New Zealand can be described as 'whole language' or 'natural language' and is an extension and development of what was, in the 1960s and 1970s, called 'language experience'. Whatever the label, and labels change as we change our perceptions, there are fixed characteristics underlying these terms which can be accurately described. The New Zealand approach includes language experience, shared reading, guided reading, independent reading—integrated with regular writing, speaking, listening, and with other subjects. Children focus on real texts and integrate their literacy skills with their growth in other areas.

Because reading is a covert mental activity, direct observation of how it occurs depends upon inference. We cannot see or measure directly what happens in the brain. Even reading aloud may not yield too many clues as to the nature of the process. For instance, oral reading errors may result from confusion at any of several points in the interface between reading for meaning and translating meanings into speech. Thus, there is inevitably some uncertainty, some room for debate and revision in our theories of how children acquire reading.

We need theory to guide our actions, but we should also be prepared to revise our theory as we learn more about the reading process — from our own observations, and the controlled studies of researchers.

Reading is a language process

Reading is basically a language process. We cannot fully understand how we learn to read without some understanding of the fundamentals of how we acquire and use language. The strategies we use in oral language — either in speaking or listening — are the same underlying strategies that we use in reading and writing. There are no mental capacities that apply only to an understanding of written language and not to speech. Without an understanding of a language we cannot read. Profoundly deaf people, who have developed a different language system from that of hearing people, find learning to read a slower and more difficult process. Thus, we begin this section with a description of language and how it is acquired.

Language is universal. Unless born with multiple impairments, everyone possesses language. The language children use may not be the language of the school, or the teacher, but it is a language nonetheless, possessing its own strengths. All languages convey meaning and all are governed by rules. There are no inferior or 'disadvantaged' languages — only language differences. The particular rules by which language is generated may differ from individual to individual, but the language is still formed by consistent rules. Sadly, some teachers often cannot avoid being judgemental about language — usually judging their own language as superior and the variant language forms of their pupils as needing correction. Children who speak minority languages are often the losers in such cases.

Language makes learning possible. It is widely agreed that we cannot think without language. Certainly, abstract thought requires words as vehicles for thinking. Language enables us to link up with the thinking and experience of other human beings. This process allows us to generate new ideas and concepts which transcend and expand our own individual thoughts. Vygotsky clearly understood this when he described learning as basically a social activity.

Oral language develops through use. As children we practise language when we talk — to others and to ourselves. We experiment with sounds, with word order and with meanings. Language is not learnt in a vacuum. We need other people around us to respond to our language.

Language develops without formal teaching. Nobody consciously teaches us our language. Parents, relatives and even some misguided teachers may hopefully try and 'teach' us adult language forms before we are ready, but the

Growth in reading builds on early language development.

sheer volume and variety of language makes systematic instruction, which tries to dictate usage, almost impossible. McNeill and his colleagues in the 1960s demonstrated the futility of 'correcting' language or trying to impose particular structures on the way young children speak with observational evidence such as this:

> *Child:* Nobody don't like me.
> *Mother:* No, say 'nobody likes me'.
> *Child:* Nobody don't like me. (eight repetitions of this dialogue)
> *Mother:* No, now listen carefully, say 'nobody likes me.'
> *Child:* Oh! Nobody don't likes me.

The mother has attempted to teach the adult form of the negative but the child is showing that he has difficulty understanding what he is being corrected for.

Language 'teaching' is more effective when it takes the form of feedback related to the content of what is being learnt rather than correction of surface grammatical features of an utterance.

Language is predictable. Say to a three-year-old: 'The cat sat on the... ?' and it is likely the reply will be 'mat'. Already the child has learnt that only certain word patterns fit into sentences. The reply 'up' or 'into' or 'sadly' will not be appropriate responses. They do not tell where the cat sat. Mature language users become very good at predicting the meaning of a speaker or an author and can often predict the exact word. Even if the exact word is not predicted usually the listener's prediction tends towards the utterance's meaning. After all, if we used too many words at random, conversation would be impossible. Fortunately, the English language is very redundant. We use more words than are necessary to convey our meanings, so missed words can be filled in from the context. Predictions are usually on the right lines.

Language acquisition is a rapid process. All around the world, children utter their first words at around one year of age, plus or minus a couple of months. In all cultures, these words tend to be familiar nouns and verbs, derived from the child's immediate experience, and in the language and dialect of the immediate family. There are, of course, large individual differences among children as to when those first words are spoken. But the patterns are universal. By eighteen months the typical child is speaking two word sentences. Vocabulary is slow to develop at first, then very rapid. At age five the child has mastered most of the regularly used syntax of his/her language, and is often speaking fluent complex sentences. Smith (1992) argues that at no other time in one's life is learning as rapid, or as effortless as when one's first language is being learnt. He states that four-year-old children learn 'about twenty new words a day.' (1992:434) Most are acquired from context, from the flow of family conversation, peer group chatter, stories read by adults or tv programmes seen. Few new words are learned as a result of deliberate teaching or consulting a dictionary. Yetta Goodman has characterised language acquisition as a balancing process between 'convention and invention'. (1992:234) The creative part of language, the unique thoughts that are being expressed are what Goodman means by invention, while convention refers to the way these thoughts are expressed so that they are intelligible to others.

As teachers we can learn much from these two important factors in language acquisition. Direct instruction, with an emphasis on specific sounds, words, and sentences, and with an emphasis on correctness of form, does not get us very far. We need to learn from the study of factors which make learning a first language so effortless. Psycholinguists such as Roger Brown (1973) have demonstrated in observational studies, that parents in the home respond naturally and predominantly to the truth of a child's utterance rather than to its form. Thus the simple behaviourist theory that parents' praise (or reinforcement) of correct speech leads to efficient language learning gets no support from real life studies. If children learned their language mainly by imitation of other's sentences, and praise from their parents, they would take years rather than months to master syntax.

With the support of sympathetic adults and one-to-one interactions language is acquired readily. Parents simplify their language, emphasise key words, speak slowly and use other facilitating devices, referred to as 'caretaker speech' or 'Motherese' and they respond naturally to what the child is trying to say.

Because oral language is learnt universally without formal teaching, schools should not, however, ignore the need to 'teach' reading. We need to define carefully what we mean by 'teach'. The school has the responsibility to set up conditions under which reading will most readily take place. The teacher must see herself as an initiator of language. A wide range of interesting print material of all kinds must be supplied, the right conditions must be provided in which children will feel willing to 'have a go', and supportive feedback must be supplied. All these conditions are part of the 'teaching' process. None of them is reducible to a standard recipe of exercises which the teacher can apply routinely without thought or skill. Children are too variable in their needs for that.

Reading is a psychological process

As we have seen, reading is a language process, but it is also a psychological process. As adults who guide this process, we need to study what goes on in children's heads while they are thinking. Psychology has many strands. Perceptual psychologists try to understand how we recognise shapes and patterns; behaviourists seek to find out how we respond to reinforcement and examine the antecedents and consequences of our behaviour; cognitive psychologists are interested in how our minds organise an understanding of the world and how we know that we know — or don't know. Each of these strands plays a part in explaining the complex process of reading. If children could not differentiate between visual shapes they could not read. If they receive inappropriate reinforcement when they open books they will not read. If they do not have some understanding of the world inside their heads, reading would be much more difficult, if not impossible.

Teachers strive to maintain an appropriate balance between the different aspects of reading illuminated by the diverse areas of psychology. No one area of psychology is able to give a complete picture of how reading occurs. Concentrating, for example, on the findings of perceptual psychologists as they study word recognition processes, is confusing means and ends. There is much more to reading than the recognition of print forms. The long-term aim of reading instruction is not the ability to recognise letters and words in isolation — it is to gain meaning from text. We suggest that laboratory experiments using artificial letter shapes and made-up words have so far done only little to show us how real children read real texts for meaning. Experiments show that we can process very familiar text more quickly than less familiar or unconnected words. They can demonstrate the value of chunking when reading and develop some insights into tunnel vision. (See Smith, 1985.)

Weaving together the various strands of psychology and linguistics has generated a new set of tools, those of psycholinguistics, by means of which we can analyse the reading process. Kenneth Goodman drew on both disciplines when he categorised reading as 'a psycholinguistic guessing game' (1976). This definition has captured the imagination of a generation of teachers because it encompassed so graphically the way in which the reader draws on a knowledge of the way language works (the linguistic part of the definition) with the psychological knowledge readers use to add to or modify their existing mental structures. The word 'guessing' has unfortunate connotations of randomness, and we know that the process is anything but random. A better term than 'guessing' would be 'prediction' which implies purposeful mental activity.

Psychologists tell us that human beings are learning all the time. Sometimes we are not even conscious that we are learning. For example, children at school quickly learn that if they smile at the teacher and look directly at her they will usually have a more positive interaction than if they do not look directly at the teacher's face and yawn while she is talking. Children learn by association — much early reading of 'environmental print' is probably of this kind. Children learn 'STOP' and 'LADIES' and 'TAXI' naturally as whole words, without deliberate strategies. The words stand out because they often serve human needs.

Frank Smith (1992) categorises the way we learn as being of two types. Either it is official learning or it is informal. *Official learning* is structured and deliberate. It takes place:

> *sporadically, and in small amounts, as a result of solitary individual effort, and when properly organised and rewarded.*

When a teacher has a class reciting a list of words which begin with 'bl' and then asks them to think of more, the children are engaged in official learning. This is learning to please the teacher and is often learning which is removed from an authentic context. Competent teachers may find ways of fostering interest in official learning tasks, but it requires external motives to make it effective.

By contrast, *informal learning* is:

> *spontaneous, continuous and effortless, requiring no particular attention, conscious motivation, or specific reinforcement; learning occurs in all kinds of situations and is not subject to forgetting. In this view learning is social rather than solitary. (Smith, 1992:432)*

Smith considers that the official type of learning predominates in reading classes and actively works against children becoming fluent readers. He was writing about North American classrooms, but we should not dismiss his analysis as completely irrelevant to New Zealand. How much of our school curriculum is fragmented into discrete units, the purposes of which escape most children?

Teachers may find it threatening to the profession that children learn informally and effortlessly many things which teachers struggle to teach — or even to discourage. Consider how easily most children learn to swear. Nobody deliberately teaches them to swear but many young children rapidly acquire an elaborate vocabulary of swear words, often in spite of the efforts of their parents and teachers. Language acquisition is truly an intriguing process.

The study of how young children learn to read, without formal teaching from professional teachers, also has much to commend itself to schools and teachers.

Studies of such early readers by Durkin (1976) in the United States, and Clark (1976), in Scotland, have shown us that many children acquire reading naturally, at home, without formal instruction, and that such children frequently go on to high achievement in their later schooling. Such accounts of reading acquisition must give pause for thought to those who believe it is best taught consciously and systematically, item by item, word by word, using extrinsic motivation.

What is 'the great debate' about learning to read?

Before presenting our preferred model for understanding the reading process, it is important to describe briefly two contrasting viewpoints which have led to a 'great debate' in a number of western countries. The debate also surfaces in New Zealand from time to time. (Tunmer, 1990; Clay, 1992; Nicholson, 1986)

One widely held theory is that reading ability consists of a hierarchy of sub-skills, which are best learned systematically by teacher modelling, regular practice and subsequent integration. This view, often referred to as the 'bottom-up' theory, assumes that the reading act is best described as one in which lower-level or perceptual processes (to do with letters and sounds) precede the higher level (meaning) processes. Hence the label, 'bottom-up'. Proponents of this view tend to promote the deliberate teaching of letters, sounds and blends to children, using flashcards, drills and brief artificial texts, until the children have automatised the decoding process, and become reasonably fluent at reading aloud. Phonics are taught both in isolation and in controlled contexts and children are believed to develop an efficient set of strategies for attacking unknown words. In Frank Smith's terms, they put their faith in official learning. Advocates of the 'bottom-up' theory claim that good readers do not guess, or predict upcoming text, but translate the visual aspects of print directly into sound, and subsequently into meaning. (Nicholson, 1986; Gough, 1980)

At the other extreme, 'top-down' theorists argue that the deliberate teaching of the basic elements (letters, sounds, blends, words) merely fragments the process, distracts the child from the real business of reading and turns reading from an enjoyable language process into an abstract and difficult task (Goodman, 1986; F Smith, 1985). Besides, as Frank Smith points out, the English language is such that word attack based on phonic approaches will be correct less than 50 per cent of the time. There are so many exceptions to English phonic rules. Teachers who follow a top-down theory avoid systematic phonic teaching, and focus on reading for meaning at all times. Children are assumed to acquire their word attack skills incidentally, while reading and rereading favourite books, repetitive texts, poems and songs.

The majority of New Zealand teachers lean more towards this position. It is referred to as the 'top-down' model, because the reader's higher mental processes are believed to precede and control the lower perceptual processes. Educators who support this model of the reading process usually advocate a 'whole language' approach to teaching, arguing that reading and writing are best acquired 'naturally' in the same way as we learn to speak and listen. Teaching methods which highlight a child's purpose and meaning from the outset, such as language experience or shared reading, with high interest books, are used as the vehicle for helping children gain these elements incidentally, by repeated exposure to interesting text, assisted by familiar context and supportive teaching — at the point of interest.

The interactive position

It is beyond the scope of this introductory chapter to examine in depth the research bases and implications of these opposing views. Suffice it to say that there is much to be said for an intermediate or interactive view which accepts that children respond to many cues, simultaneously, or successively when they are reading. At different times, readers are responding to cues from the print, the meaning, and the syntax. They respond to the letters they see, especially at the beginning and ends of words; they respond to the shape of the word, common suffixes and other recurring spelling patterns. They also respond to the rhyme, the pictures, their memory for the story, or to assistance from a helpful adult or peer. These various cues interact to help the child achieve a successful understanding of the author's message, and by mutual interaction help him/her build up a repertoire of strategies for doing so efficiently and independently in future. Some children are more sensitive to letter cues, some to meaning cues, some to syntax. They have their compensatory strengths and weaknesses. By this theory one learns to read by reading — by practising these interactive strategies in meaningful and interesting contexts. Thus, phonic associations are learned by the child, in context, to achieve the child's purpose, and are practised in use.

Such an interactive position provides a useful basis for thinking about how best to help children into reading — and it is accepted by many researchers and teachers. However, it is incomplete without some consideration of the wider social influences on our reading practices.

These three categories of influence — linguistic, psychological and social — are not discrete categories. They clearly overlap and influence one another. An overarching theory (including linguistic, psychological and social factors) which should help us to integrate them effectively can be found in the work of Vygotsky.

What was Vygotsky's viewpoint?

Although Vygotsky died in 1934 the significance of his work has only gradually been realised in the last decade in the West. We believe it provides a very helpful theoretical perspective on reading. Amongst Vygotsky's key ideas were his zone of proximal development and the belief that our higher mental functioning derives from our social life. His concept of the zone of proximal development was discussed earlier on page 6. This zone is critical in understanding how children progress, from a stage where they stumble and fail with a text to a stage where they are just able to master it.

Vygotsky claimed that:

> 'the only good kind of instruction is that which marches ahead of development and leads it; it must be aimed not so much at the ripe as the ripening function.' (p 104)

Tharp and Gallimore (1988), in an influential interpretation of Vygostsky, have identified four stages of the zone of proximal development. Stage one occurs when performance is assisted by more capable others. In this stage the child has a very limited capacity to understand the task to be accomplished and relies heavily on another person to assist in the performance of the task. At first, the child is completely dependent on the more capable person. Tharp and Gallimore (1988) comment that:

> ordinarily this understanding develops through conversation during the task performance. When some conception of the overall performance has been acquired through language or other semiotic processes, the child can be assisted by other means — questions, feedback and further cognitive structuring. (1988:33)

For example, the teacher may say to the preschooler, 'Let's read this story. Where shall we begin? What do you think the story is about?' The teacher here is structuring the experience — approaching the story in an orderly fashion and giving the child ways to systematically approach the book.

Bruner (1983) coined the phrase 'handover principle' to refer to the lessening of assistance from the expert person to the learner. What happens during the handover phases is that the mental functioning which occurred as a result of the social interaction between, say, the skilled reader and a novice, is now becoming internalised in the mind of the novice. To use Vygotsky's term there has been 'a shift from the interpsychological to the intrapsychological.' The role of the expert is to structure the situation. A teacher does this by providing certain books, and not others, for her new entrant class. Gradually, as the need for scaffolding decreases, and the handover phase becomes more marked, children also take over the responsibility for structuring the situation themselves. Thus, children no longer have to be confined to one section of the library from which to choose their books — they can roam freely through all the shelves and choose their own books. The handover principle is clearly illustrated, too, in the shared book method.

Stage two of the zone of proximal development is reached when performance is assisted by the learner. Stage two does not mean that the process is fully automatic or that it does not require conscious control. It still does. The difference between stage one and stage two is that assistance now comes primarily from the self. For example, Holdaway (1972) describes a number of strategies a child can use when a word is not understood in a sentence. Included in these problem-solving strategies are:

> Read-on: *miss out the word and go on to the end of the*
>   *sentence*
> Re-run: *stop and go back to the beginning of the sentence*
> Picture: *look at the illustrations in the light of the developing*
>   *sentence*
> Compare: *compare with a familiar word — prefixes, and root words.*
> (1972:109)

When readers consciously invoke one of these strategies, they are aware that they need assistance but in this case the assistance is coming from their own inner voice. Control and guidance have now passed from another person to the learner. Reading is becoming a self regulating process. As adults we rely on inner voice to direct our activities when faced with new or novel situations.

Stage three is described as that stage 'where performance is developed, automatised and 'fossilized''. Now the task is carried out without any conscious effort. It has become automatic and external assistance is no longer needed. What was a strategy used by the helpful adult has now become internalised. In fact, outside assistance may be irritating and unhelpful. Consider the experienced car driver whose passengers read aloud each road sign as it is approached. Most drivers soon inform their passengers in very clear and forceful language that they can read and act on the stop sign or the caution sign that is approaching without any prompting from their passengers. Learning is no longer developing — it has happened. The term 'fossilization' is used by Vygotsky, according to Tharp and Gallimore, to emphasise not only that development has ceased but also to emphasise the fixity of the action and its distance 'from the social and mental forces of change.' (1988:38)

Sometimes, if the skill is not practised, de-automatisation of performance can occur, causing a regression back through the zone of proximal development. Stage four has now been reached. Nothing we ever learn is permanently fixed. Changes in lifestyle, personal upheavals, or illness mean that we forget and need to be retaught. The three stages described above are then repeated. Confronted with a baffling page to read — for example, the instructions that comes with kit-set furniture — the fluent adult reader will often revert to reading aloud the instructions in a desperate attempt to understand how to assemble the piece of furniture. Thus, there has been a reversion to using the inner voice in an effort to understand. If this fails, the neighbours can be called upon to act as experts and provide the scaffolding which should lead to the furniture being successfully assembled.

Society and reading

Humankind is a social species. We live in families, with partners, with friends, with other people. We congregate in villages, towns and cities. People who live by themselves are often stigmatised as 'loners' or 'anti-social'. Furthermore we are constantly influenced by other people and their actions.

What is written, what is published for a wider audience, who reads it and for what purposes are all determined by people in our society. Each society differs and has different expectations of reading and of literacy. The way a liberation theologian in a New York theological college reads and interprets the Bible will differ from the way a devout Moslem reads the Koran in Mecca. The role that print plays in the daily lives of a Solomon Islander will differ from that of a Wall Street banker or a Wellington politician. What is regarded as fit and proper reading, for adults as well as for children, differs from society to society and even within groups in each society. Do we, for example, include comics as appropriate reading material for children in our society? How do we view the reading involved in a computer game? Do we expect our children to read abstract religious tracts? The answers to such questions differ from one society to another, from one family to another, and help explain differences in reading habits and attainment.

Vygotsky's four-stage explanation provides a bridge between society and the individual. Earlier theoretical accounts of the reading process failed to explain the role that the traditions and expectations of society played in an individual's becoming literate. Similarly, the important role of the teacher has often been ignored in theoretical accounts of learning to read. Now we are well on the way towards a more coherent theory which explains both the role of society and teacher and the ways in which they interact with the child's growing mastery of the reading process.

Pulling it all together

To describe a specific act of reading — say, an eight-year-old reading a Part Two Journal story — would involve drawing on knowledge from all the disciplines we have mentioned. Just as it is possible to describe riding a bicycle by referring to the laws of physics and still not be able to ride a bike when given one, so it is with reading. Fluent reading, like riding a bicycle, is a dynamic process which simultaneously draws on knowledge from a wide range of sources without the reader consciously knowing it is happening. Just as the bicycle rider automatically adjusts for minor wind gusts, differing road surfaces, and the particular effort required of the legs as the pedals are cranked around, so does the reader automatically draw from a range of strategies while reading. In fact the only time the bicycle rider is conscious of what is required is when things go wrong, which usually results in a collision between rider and road. And, in a parallel fashion, the reader usually becomes conscious of reading strategies only when a passage is not understood and when reading stops — the equivalent action to falling off your bicycle.

Here is our eight-year-old, Catherine, in Standard 2 at the local school settling down to read 'Daylight Saving Time' by Jane Buxton (School Journal, Part Two, Number Two, 1993). The session is being taken by the teacher with a group of five children as part of a guided silent reading lesson. The story is about a little girl who builds a city in her sandpit. Her parents call her to come to bed, even though it is still daylight. She protests, but her parents explain that it is daylight saving time, and the clocks have been changed. In bed she is visited by the tiny mayor of the city she has made, who asks her to come out and finish making the town clock. She does so and finds the town populated by tiny people. The story ends with the little girl determined to stay up the following night and visit her sandpit town again after dark.

Catherine knows a lot about language although she would be hard-pressed to explain that knowledge. She can use language for a variety of aims and in a number of ways. She knows that language has a definite order and that the order affects meaning. She knows that words have multiple meanings and that context determines what meanings are selected. She knows a lot about written language — that it is made up from letters, which can be distinguished one from another, words, sentences, paragraphs and stories. She knows that print is read in an orderly fashion from left to right along the lines and down the page, from top to bottom.

Some of this knowledge may be the result of direct official teaching, but most of it has been learnt informally as a result of being bathed in a sea of language since she was a small child. Even these elementary learnings are a result of interacting psychological processes. To be aware that 'b' is a different letter from 'd' depends on the concepts the brain has learnt that this shape 'b' is different from this shape 'd' — so she responds differently and the difference has filtered through her visual perceptual system. It is more than visual perception. Visual perception is driven by what the brain instructs the eye to see. Catherine has learnt to discriminate between letters, and between words by many repeated exposures to print, since she was a baby, firstly through stories read at home, then through a constant diet of reading and writing when she began school.

Of equal importance to her knowledge of letters, words and sentences is her expectation that the story she is about to read will make sense. She will be able to understand both what is happening to the people in the story and that it all fits together. She expects the experience to have meaning. The eight years she has lived have given her a mental framework, an elaborate set of schema, around which to structure experiences — either real experiences or vicarious ones like reading. In order to do this, the story needs to contain elements of familiarity — we can work out what a unicorn is like because we have an idea of what a goat is and we can extrapolate from there to a small goat-like creature with a single horn in the centre of its head — unlike a goat which will have two horns on either side of its head. This story switches from reality to fantasy and the teacher may have to provide the scaffolding, either before Catherine reads or after, to allow her to understand the switch the author makes between the two worlds.

From this account it can be seen that reading is not a passive process of recognising letters, words, phrases, sentences and paragraphs. It is an active process which begins with a desire to make sense of what is in front of the reader. The active process involves the reader moving from her knowledge about the content of the story to her knowledge of how language works, to her knowledge of the conventions of print. Such shifts in attention may occur many times during her reading of the story. The reader has to pull it all together to read the story. Only she can do it. Nobody can do it for her. Children learn to read themselves; direct teaching plays only a minor role.

How does Catherine know when to call on these different strategies? When the reading ceases to make sense. In other words, when what is being read no longer conforms to what the reader expects to be happening. Then a hierarchy of strategies is called upon.

If Catherine is reading aloud, the sequence of events is — from print to meaning to sounds. She sees the print, constructs the meaning, then produces the sounds. This is a significant, and some researchers, such as Gough and Nicholson, would argue, a controversial order. In the model of proficient reading that we accept, meaning is paramount. Once meaning has been attributed to the print, oral language can be supplied if reading aloud is necessary. Even experienced television newsreaders will scan a news item before they read it aloud on television. Oral reading should follow meaning; it does not precede it. When children read a miscue, such as 'sleeping' for 'asleep', this is a result of the meaning being understood and then recoded in the vocabulary the reader normally uses. Similarly, the child who reads 'forest' instead of 'woods' in the sentence 'Red Riding Hood ran through the woods' has understood the meaning but is unconsciously substituting a word used more commonly in her oral repertoire. A more spectacular example is the Standard 1 boy taught by the author who substituted 'chook' consistently for 'hen' when reading aloud *The Little Red Hen*.

Catherine is part of a group which is interacting with the teacher. Both the group and the teacher have expectations of what is going to happen. They have an established schema for reading lessons. They expect to listen to the teacher set the scene for the story they are about to read; they expect to read the story without being hit or punched by either the teacher or their classmates, and Catherine expects to be able to discuss what she has read with her mates in the group when she has finished reading. Just as Catherine is part of a group so the group is part of a class which has expectations about reading. Because the class is Standard 2, the children expect to be reading Journals, and they are aware that Part Two Journals are more advanced and signify more competence in reading than Part One Journals. They also expect to be reading 'chapter' books which, again in the eyes of eight-year-olds, have more status than 'baby' books.

The class is part of a school which in turn has expectations about reading. The value the school puts on its library and the resources allocated to it, together with a coherent plan running through the whole school for teaching reading, again influences each child's expectations. Catherine is also part of a family. The value her parents place on reading — whether it is an activity which her parents often do at home and are seen to be doing by Catherine, will influence her attitude to reading. The occupation, education levels, and expectations of her parents will influence her approach to reading. All this adds up to the social context of learning to read, which has a powerful influence in learning to read.

The teacher has structured the setting by allocating this particular story to be read. She has also designated the members of the group. Her actions in discussing daylight saving ('Are there extra hours in the day? What happens when we change the time on the clocks?') provide scaffolding by which the children can grasp the multi-layered nature of this story.

After the teacher has set the scene for reading, the group read the story silently. The teacher moves away to work with another group. When she has finished reading Catherine turns to her neighbour and says, 'Dumb story, I still don't get the bit about daylight saving time.' Her neighbour replies, 'Yeah, but wouldn't it be neat to have cute little people in your sandpit.'

Both readers are concerned with their understanding of the story as a whole. Catherine has reacted negatively to the fantasy element of the story — which is the part her neighbour liked. These are individual reactions to the story, based on both girls' backgrounds. Both reactions are valid — nobody has to like or enjoy everything they read. When the teacher returns to the group she asks about the daylight saving time. Several children are confused about the loss or creation of an extra hour of time and there is a lengthy discussion about what happens to the clocks twice a year. The group are more interested in pursuing this idea than the author's sub-theme of imaginary people living in the sandpit. Gradually, the idea that daylight saving time does not alter the number of hours in a day becomes clear to the group. Learning has taken place in a social context — the group grasp the concepts and then individuals internalise them. When the teacher asks Catherine why the father in the story dislikes getting up when daylight saving begins, and Catherine successfully answers the question, the teacher is satisfied that the concepts illustrated in the story have been internalised.

Figure 3 on page 89 summarises what we have written about. It shows what happens during reading. At the centre is the prime task — to construct meaning from the author's message. Around this prime task and feeding into it are a number of strategies the reader calls on. Fluent reading is automatic. Just as the proficient car driver knows when to change gears, and often does so without conscious planning, so the fluent reader invokes a range of strategies. Some strategies do require conscious effort. To ask for help from other readers requires the knowledge that understanding has broken down to the point where it is best retrieved by an appeal to another reader. Prediction from prior knowledge, or from syntax, or story grammar is a result of previous exposure to large amounts of print over time and usually does not require conscious effort to be invoked. We deliberately use the word 'prediction' in contrast to Goodman's term 'guessing', because prediction has connotations of purposeful behaviour which is built on previous learning. Guessing, on the other hand, suggests random behaviour. There is no evidence to suggest that children's reading behaviour is random. The reason for a particular oral response by a child may not always be immediately understood by a teacher, without in-depth investigations, but it is not a random utterance.

The reader

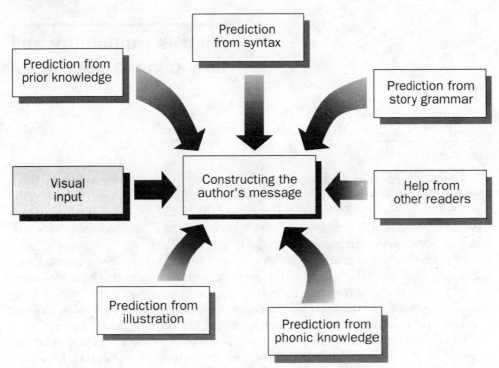

Figure 3 Diverse cues for constructing meaning - Interactive model

The chart is not meant to prescribe a set of teaching skills. Rather, during teaching episodes any one or several of these strategies may be invoked and demonstrated by the teacher. Such questions as 'what do you think the picture is trying to show us about the story?' or 'What do we know about daylight saving time?' will allow for the use of different strategies in a meaningful context.

Chapter 8

What is readability and how can we assess it?

We have argued that children learn best when they are operating at their appropriate level of difficulty, at that point when they can achieve success with some adult guidance. To help children find that level, their zone of proximal development in reading, many teachers become expert at assessing the difficulty level of books and journal stories which their children are exposed to. They note the kind of vocabulary, whether it is simple and concrete, or abstract and technical. They note the length of the sentences, the complexity of the style, the use of personal pronouns, the inclusion of visual aids and other supports to help children master the text. Teachers also take note of the interest level of the content, and whether the topic is familiar to the child. If the book or story deals with an unfamiliar theme, or lacks interest, adopts an impersonal or theoretical approach, or if it contains long sentences and a heavy vocabulary load, the teacher may recommend that the child try something else, lest she/he become bored or frustrated and so lose interest in reading. Many children are turned off reading simply because they rarely experience success with it. A good teacher, then, must be sensitive to the reading difficulty, or readability of text. Not all teachers have the time or ability to make accurate assessments of readability, and much effort has gone into assisting them on this task. Most children need guidance too, in choosing suitable book levels, and so do librarians, newspaper reporters and advertisers.

There are many objective ways of assessing readability. Overseas researchers have come up with no fewer than fifty objective systems, and several are in common use in New Zealand schools. Some of the more

Choosing the right book.

common methods are briefly outlined below. They are recommended here only as a guide, to be used with due caution about their limitations.

Fry readability method

This method was developed in the United States by Edward Fry. It is based on the assumption that the major difficulties that children experience when reading a text can be detected by such symptoms as long sentences and long words. Therefore to estimate the readability of a text one needs to count the average length of the sentences and the average length of the words in the text. The latter component is measured by counting the number of syllables per 100 words, which is a simpler but coarser measure of word length than the number of actual letters per word.

Thus, the technique requires the following steps:

1   From the book or story to be assessed, select three passages of 100 words at random.

2   Count the number of syllables in each passage and record them.

3   Count the number of sentences in each passage and record them.

4   Calculate the average of the three passages, for syllables and for sentences. If the three estimates are very different it is advised that a fourth passage be rated, and included in the average.

5   Look up the accompanying Fry Readability Table to locate the point which corresponds to the two indicators, for syllables and for sentences. This point indicates the American grade level.

6   Convert these grade levels to an approximate reading age level by adding on five years (ie, the age of children in the year before they begin school in Grade 1 in the United States).

The method is relatively quick and easy to use. However, the assumption that polysyllabic words are more difficult than words of one syllable is not always true. Children probably have less trouble with 'elephant' and 'alligator' than they have with 'chance' or 'truth'. Nevertheless, a close study of word frequency counts shows that it is a fair guide on average, and when three or four passages are used, the exceptions balance out. Young children's books do have many short words and short sentences. Scientific and legal documents tend to have long words and complex sentences. Of course, the method takes no account of the reader's interest or background knowledge, and is sometimes inaccurate.

To illustrate the method the first 100 words from *The Hitchhikers' Guide to the Galaxy* are assessed on page 92. The excerpt has four sentences (marked with a double slash) and 125 syllables. (Words with two or more syllables are marked with a single slash.) If two or more passages were rated at the same level, the book would be assessed at Grade 8 level or at a reading age of thirteen years.

The house stood on a slight rise just on the edge of the vill/age// . It stood on its own and looked out ov/er a broad spread of West Count/ry farm/land// . Not a re/mark/ab/le house by an/y means – it was a/bout thirt/y years old, squat/tish, squar/ish, made of brick, and had four windows set in front, of a size and pro/por/tion which more or less e/xact/ly failed to please the eye//. The on/ly per/son for whom the house was in an/y way spe/cial was Ar/thur Dent, and that was on/ly be/cause it happened to be the one he lived in//. (100 words)

A useful method for assessing classroom materials

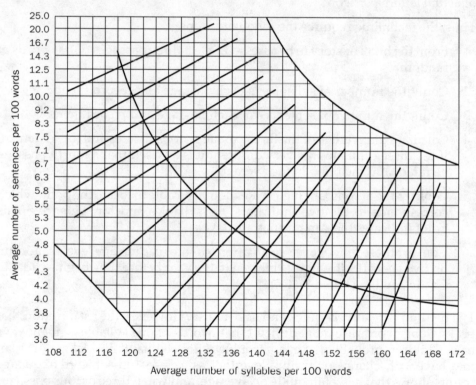

Graph adopted to give *reading level* (years), instead of American grade level (class)

Figure 4 Fry Readability Graph

Noun frequency method

Rationale

This method was developed by Elley (1975) for New Zealand conditions and has been revised by Elley and Croft (1989). Essentially, it is a measure of vocabulary load, worked out by empirical means, using examples of text of varying difficulty, drawn from adult encyclopedias, newspapers, popular magazines and children's books.

After comparing the accuracy of several methods — using counts of sentence length, abstract words, prepositional phrases, syllables per 100 words and various methods of assessing vocabulary difficulty — Elley found that a measure of the familiarity of the content words (nouns, verbs, adjectives) in the text to be read was a consistently accurate and efficient indicator of how difficult the prose was for children. The other methods were less consistent in sorting passages in the same rank order of difficulty as teachers did. Using a word count of the most common words in children's writing (Arvidson, 1960), Elley (1975) found that a measure of the familiarity of the nouns in the passage correlated 0.9 with the average of teachers' and pupils' subjective judgements of the same passages. The same trend was found in five separate research studies (see Elley and Croft, 1989). The rationale is explained in more detail in that publication, along with other evidence of its validity. Nouns appear to carry the main burden of the author's message. If they are familiar to the reader the passage is likely to be comprehensible.

Method

To assess the difficulty level of a story or of another piece of writing, teachers (or anyone else curious about the difficulty level) should take the following steps:

1   Select three passages long enough to contain twenty-five different nouns in each. If textbooks are to be rated, it is normal to select initially from the early chapters. Otherwise the passages may be selected at random, from the beginning, middle and end.

2   Identify each word in the passage to be rated.

3   Look up the level of each noun in the Noun Frequency List. This is based on Arvidson's graded spelling list (1970) supplemented by Croft's word count (see *Set*, 1983). The levels range from Level 1 (common) to Level 8 (rare). Any noun not on the list is rated at Level 9. For example, some ratings are: ball(1); ballet(7); ballad(9).

4   For each selection rated, calculate the mean frequency level — ie, add up the level numbers and divide by the number of nouns.

5   Take the average of the three selections.

6   Consult the following table to obtain the approximate reading age of the material rated.

Mean Noun Frequency	Approximate Reading Age
Below 2.8	7–8 years
2.8 to 3.2	7.5 to 8.5
3.2 to 3.6	8 to 9
3.6 to 4.0	8.5 to 9.5
4.0 to 4.4	9 to 10
4.4 to 4.8	9.5 to 10.5
4.8 to 5.2	10 to 12
5.2 to 5.6	11 to 13
5.6 to 6.0	12 to 14
6.0 to 6.4	13 to 16
Over 6.4	15 and over

Reproduced with permission from *Assessing the Difficulty of Reading Materials: The Noun Frequency Method–Revised Edition* by Warwick B. Elley and A. Cedric Croft, New Zealand Council for Educational Research, 1989.

Note:
(a)   If a noun occurs more than once in a passage, count it only once.
(b)   Do not count people's names.
(c)   All other proper nouns (days, ethnic groups, countries, institutions) follow the same rules as common nouns (eg, Monday (2) Maori (2)).
(d)   Plurals are given the same rating as singular nouns.

Like the Fry Readability technique, the Noun Frequency method provides only an estimate, which will usually be correct within one level. With ordinary prose, journals, newspapers, magazines, children's books, it is quite easy to calculate for those who know their nouns — and has been used extensively in New Zealand. The 1989 revision is also available on computer disk from the New Zealand Council for Educational Research. However, its dependence on a measure of familiarity means that it is unsuitable for estimating the readability of technical text, or any prose which uses a lot of highly specialised vocabulary. It is also unreliable for assessing poetry, or for very short texts containing fewer than twenty-five nouns.

Like all other formulae, it cannot take account of the reader's interest in the material, or their prior knowledge. It will also underestimate the difficulty of text which contains a high density of new or abstract ideas. An example of its use is given in Figure 5.

Selection from New Zealand School Journal (Part 3, Number 3 1986).

THE LIMPET MYSTERY

When you were a small <u>limpet</u>, you found this <u>rock</u>. Between <u>tides</u>, you were always in this exact <u>spot</u>. I watched you grow to fit the <u>bumps</u> and <u>hollows</u> till there were no <u>gaps</u> between your <u>shell</u> and the rock. I think if there were gaps, you would dry out and die. This rock you are on is not very hard. Your shell has worn an oval <u>groove</u> in it.

When the tide is in, you are like a <u>sheep</u> slowly chewing your <u>way</u> around the rock, grazing on <u>algae</u> and tiny <u>seaweeds</u>. The fastest you move is about one <u>centimetre</u> a <u>minute</u>. I have measured and timed you.

When the tide starts going out, you turn and race for <u>home</u> (limpet <u>racing</u>, that is) at nearly three centimetres a minute. Before the rock dries out, you must be back in your oval groove. If you don't make it, you may not be able to seal yourself to the rock. You might dry out and die. You always make it.

How do you find your way back if you have no <u>eyes</u> to see the way? I thought maybe you were following your <u>scent</u> back. I scrubbed your <u>trail</u> with a scrubbing <u>brush</u>. You still got back.

I put <u>bricks</u> in your <u>path</u>. You went around them. You went over them. I put a <u>cage</u> over your home. After two <u>days</u>, you seemed to forget. You stopped trying to get back. I took away the cage and lifted you back to your <u>place</u>.

limpet	9	groove	9	eyes	1
rock	3	sheep	2	scent	9
tides	7	way	1	trail	5
spot	4	algae	9	brush	3
bumps	5	seaweeds	8	bricks	5
hollows	9	centimetre	4	path	5
gaps	6	minute	2	cage	3
shell	5	home	1	days	1
		racing	5	place	1
				TOTAL:	122

Average frequency level of nouns = 122/26 = 4.69.

This passage would be classified as suitable for average $9^{1}/_{2} - 10^{1}/_{2}$ year old readers.

Figure 5 Worked example, Noun frequency method. Reproduced with permission from *Assessing the Difficulty of Reading Materials: The Noun Frequency Method–Revised Edition* by Warwick B. Elley and A. Cedric Croft, New Zealand Council for Educational Research, 1989.

Cloze technique

Another method of assessing readability is provided by the cloze technique, developed by an American, Wilson Taylor (1953), for rating newspaper and magazine articles. Taylor devised a simple procedure in which every fifth word is deleted from the passage to be rated and replaced with a blank of standard length. If a reader is able to fill in the missing words with 40–45 per cent accuracy she/he can read the passage with understanding. Such a reader is able to make use of the context and understands the writer's message, vocabulary and use of syntax to predict reasonably accurately the missing words. The reader is 'in tune' with the writer.

Compare the following two sentences:

1   *When the three bears returned home they _____ very surprised to find _____ their front door was wide _____.*

2   *It is surely not accidental that _____ all attempts to simulate humour _____ by computer have required some type of _____ memory.*

The first sentence is taken from a well-known story. The vocabulary is familiar and the syntax is simple. Therefore, the blanks are relatively easy to fill in (ie, were, that, open). The second sentence is from a psychology textbook. It deals with relatively unfamiliar contents, uses less common vocabulary and has complex structure. The reader would therefore be expected to have more difficulty completing the blanks (ie, virtually, behaviour, working).

Of course it takes more than three blanks to produce a reliable result. The recommended procedure for establishing readability by the cloze method is as follows:

1   Randomly select three passages of at least 110 words from the story to be rated. With textbooks the passages should normally be taken from the first three chapters.

2   Delete every fifth word, after the first line, and replace it with a blank of standard length.

3   Prepare the passage in the form of a test with suitable directions and an example to ensure students know what to do.

4   Ask the children to read the passages and fill in the blanks from context — one word for each blank.

5   Mark the children's responses accepting only the author's original word as correct. (While synonyms may indicate a high degree of understanding by the child, the theoretical basis of the method assumes that reader is more in tune with the author's intentions if the exact word is chosen, and the criterion for readability requires it.)

6   If the score obtained is 45 per cent or better, the passage is sufficiently comprehensible by the child that it can be understood well enough to learn

from independently. Below 40 per cent it is probably too hard and the child would need help.

The cloze technique has been validated by several American researchers (Bormuth, 1969; Rankin, 1969) and is sometimes used by book publishers to establish an average level of difficulty for textbooks. Elley (1976, 1981) showed that it correlated well with other measures of readability of materials and reading ability of students. He also showed that many high school students are expected to read textbooks which are beyond their comprehension level. Over half of the students in a typical third form classes had scores below 40 per cent on texts designed for their use.

The cloze procedure takes longer to apply than most other methods, but it has the advantage that it can be used with technical material, that can and does, to some extent, reflect the prior knowledge of student readers. If they score well on a cloze test they probably have sufficient background schema related to the content and know the vocabulary of the text well enough that they can make good inferences about the topic of the text.

Conclusion

We have outlined three common procedures for assessing readability — the Fry method, the Noun Frequency count and the Cloze technique. Each has its limitations, and some critics question the value of any objective attempt to assess readability at all. It is alleged that no such method can take account of readers' interests or purposes, that they overlook such intangibles as the conceptual load, the use of cohesive ties and the density of ideas. This is only partially true. Conceptual load, for instance, is not measured directly, but the high correlations found between different estimates of readability suggest that it is assumed indirectly. Unfamiliar concepts are usually couched in unfamiliar terms, and these are measured by the Noun Frequency and the Cloze procedures. Interest level cannot be directly assessed, but this is acknowledged, and needs to be part of the decision about suitability of materials.

In the end it is an empirical question. Many studies have shown that these readability assessments are valid in normal circumstances. Many teachers have also found them helpful in selecting books and guiding children. Therefore, they are offered as another aid to teachers, pupils and librarians, to be used where they are felt to be useful. For those who have the time and ability to judge readability without such aids, they are welcome to manage without.

Chapter 9

Assessment in reading

Why assess?

Good teachers make a habit of assessing their pupils' progress in reading, frequently and informally. Every time a teacher hears seven-year-old Jonathan read aloud in a group, or observes him choosing a book, or watches him absorbed in a comic, or listens to him talk about his favourite author — in all these situations she is making informal assessments, which may guide her decisions about how best to understand and to extend Jonathan's reading. If teachers are to keep children working close to their level of challenge, close to their zone of proximal development, they need to know how well they are coping with material of different levels of difficulty. Good teaching also requires some recording of these regular observations so that they are not overlooked or forgotten when planning future programmes for Jonathan, or when reporting to Jonathan's parents.

Sometimes, however, more structured and formal assessments are warranted. The Principal may call for a class survey of reading achievement levels; the Ministry of Education may want evidence of current reading abilities; the Special Education Service may want a formal assessment of a few pupils; a curriculum evaluation may call for information on changes in children's attitudes, or the volume of reading done; or a decision is needed on which children to select for a special programme.

Any decision about which assessment procedures to use should be guided by a consideration of the reliability and validity of the procedures. *Reliability* means the consistency of the measure. If the same or a similar testing procedure is given after an extended period of time, or by another person, we would expect the results to be similar if the procedure is reliable. The results should be accurate. On the other hand, *validity* refers to the relevance of a test for a particular purpose. For instance, it is not usually a valid measure of reading to test words in isolation when very little of what we read consists of isolated words. If most reading at an intermediate school is silent, a test of oral reading is unlikely to be a valid measure. A valid test should then, serve the teacher's intended purpose. It should not distort a child's ability because of cultural or gender bias in the questions. Nor should results be affected by undue time pressure, or complicated directions, or unfamiliar test format.

There are many purposes for assessing children's reading. Some purposes are 'low stakes', provisional, and of temporary interest only to the teacher and pupil. Others are 'high stakes', important for future decisions about the pupil, and require more formal tests and standardised testing conditions. This chapter begins by spelling out a number of widely acknowledged purposes for assessing children's reading abilities, describes the implications of these various purposes for the form of assessment, and outlines some of the more commonly used tests and other procedures used for assessment.

Some assessments can be made by informal observation.

Table 2 on page 100 lists on the left hand side some major purposes for assessing children's reading. While most are designed ultimately to improve pupil learning, some of these purposes do so only indirectly, and a few are more concerned with the official need for accountability. These various purposes cannot all be achieved in the same way. The second column in the table indicates that assessment is best undertaken early in the year for some purposes, later in the year for others. Some purposes lead to important decisions for a child or a school, others are 'low stakes' affecting only a temporary judgement, readily revised after further observation. Such differences in the stakes inevitably give rise to different kinds of assessment methods, and levels of reliability, and formality, as indicated in the right hand columns of the table.

Thus, for daily planning decisions, regular observation of children at work from the beginning of the year, makes for better judgement about what materials and tasks are appropriate for children, how closely to observe them, how much help to give, when to probe further and when to change activities. These

Purpose	Time of year	High or low stakes	Typical methods	Level of reliability needed
1 Daily planning	Daily	Low	Observation Discussion	Medium
2 Diagnosis of difficulties	Early and often	Low	Running records Informal reading inventories	Medium to High
3 Grouping for reading	Early	Medium	Group tests	Medium
4 Matching children with materials	Any time	Low	Standardised tests	Medium
5 Promotion to next class	End of year	High	Running records Standardised tests	High
6 Reporting on individuals to parents	End of term	Medium	Classroom tests	High
7 Reporting on groups to Ministry, ERO	On request	High	Standardised tests	Medium to High
8 School-leaving awards	End of year	High	Internal or external exams	High

Table 2 Some purposes and characteristics of assessment in reading/language

decisions are low stakes, of interest largely to teacher and child. By contrast, formal testing for promotion decisions, or for reporting to parents or boards of trustees, or ERO officials may require a formal test, long enough to be reliable, given and marked under carefully standardised conditions, and capable of interpretation in relation to national norms or clearly prescribed standards.

Types of assessments

Not all reading assessments tell the same story. Some children know their letters and sounds, but do not read for meaning; some comprehend well, but cannot cope with library skills; some have extensive vocabularies but are unhappy reading aloud; some show excellent word recognition but do not feel positive about reading.

Thus, it is important to know the strengths and limitations of a variety of assessment techniques, and to know what may be expected from each. The major kinds of assessment techniques are therefore listed below:

1   Informal observation.

2   Running records.

3   Informal reading inventories.

4   Tests of word recognition.

5   Tests of silent reading comprehension.

6   Tests of vocabulary.

7   Diagnostic survey.

8   Amount of reading.

9   Attitudes to reading.

10   Tests of study skills.

Informal observation

At all class levels children can be observed reading silently, choosing books, talking about books, listening to shared reading, writing book reports, using a library catalogue, reading to another child. Regular informal observations form the basis of judgement for most pupils, but such observations need to be recorded if they are to be of most value. Children's behaviour does vary, from day to day, and a small number of observations may introduce a subjective bias or stereotype which long outlasts or misrepresents the few occasions when it was seen. In other words, casual observation may be unreliable. However, it can provide timely information about children's attitudes and skills unable to be picked up any other way.

Running records

One useful kind of systematic observation of children's reading is the running record (Clay, 1985). In the early stages of reading, running records, or 'miscue' (error) analyses (Goodman & Burke, 1972), are ideal for checking on the accuracy of individual children's reading of a given text, and for monitoring the strategies they typically adopt. No other technique reveals so clearly the extent to which children use cues of meaning, or syntax, or the grapho-phonic features of text. In the hands of a skilled teacher a running record can tell a great deal about the strategies the child uses in coping with print.

Most teachers in the junior school try to give their pupils such an assessment once a term. Slower readers will be given one more often. These records are individual assessments, given to one child at a time, so they are quite time consuming — up to thirty minutes per child in high stakes situation. However, a confirmation check on the child's current book can be completed in ten minutes or so. As the child develops fluency in reading, and shows evidence of good comprehension, the need for running records is diminished. Competent readers in the middle school rarely need to be assessed this way.

For regular monitoring, in a low stakes situation, a teacher may ask the child to read aloud from his/her current reading book, a sample of 100 to 150 words. As the child reads, the teacher will make a running record, on a blank sheet of paper, recording a tick for every word read correctly, and recording each error or miscue according to a set of conventions (listed below). The teacher will note all the observable reading behaviour — omissions, substitutions, directional confusions, self-corrections and pauses, and make notes on any other unusual behaviour. This record forms the basis for an objective analysis of the child's reading strategies.

For more important decisions, such as for promotion to another class or selection for Reading Recovery, it is important to use both seen and unseen texts, ranging from easy to difficult (ie, passages with reading accuracy levels of more than 95 per cent correct, to those with less than 90 per cent). Thus, three or four different passages may be required.

Dr Marie Clay designed the procedures for conducting such records during the 1970s, and her manuals are recommended for those who wish to know more (Clay, 1985). While she was constructing and refining the technique, the Goodmans were simultaneously developing, in the United States, the miscue analysis, which essentially achieves the same ends, using different conventions (Goodman & Burke, 1972). For the miscue analysis, the teacher records miscues (or errors) on a duplicate copy of the child's text. No ticks are required for correct responses. Miscue analyses also will typically require pupils to retell what they have read, or respond to questions. The subsequent analyses of the two techniques are similar, however.

In both procedures, teachers will normally calculate and record:

1   the percentage of words correctly read (ie, the child's *accuracy*);
2   the proportion of *self-corrections* of incorrect responses;

3   the proportion of miscues that are *semantically acceptable* (which make meaningful sense in the context);
4   the proportion of miscues which are *syntactically acceptable* (which fit grammatically in the sentence);
5   the proportion of miscues which show the child is using *visual cues* (eg, which begin or end with the same letters);
6   the proportion of miscues which show the child is responding to *sound cues* (eg, which have the same initial or final sound as the target word).

Susan — Running record — Term 1 — Week 6

What goes up?

What goes up?
I go up, a ball goes up,
a bird goes up, a kite goes up,
a helicopter goes up, *aeroplane* & a an aeroplane goes up,
and a rocket goes up fast.
Appeal – "you try it!"

Come and Look

Come and look at Susan
Come and look at Bill Black's helicopter.
Come and look at Daddy.
Come and look at Susan's cat. *pussy cat*
Come and look at Mummy.
Come and look at Daddy digging.
Come and look at Susan's painting.
Come and look at Susan's elephant.

Results

Number of running words = 78

Number of errors = 3

Error rate = $\dfrac{RW}{E}$ = 1:26

Accuracy – 100 – $(\dfrac{E}{RW} \times \dfrac{100}{1})$%   96%

Number of self-corrections   1

Self correction rate = $\dfrac{E+SC}{SC}$ 1:4

Comment

At this stage, Susan is displaying sound early reading skills. Her errors do not affect the sense of the passages, and she is self-correcting when her words do not match the picture. The errors 'a aeroplane' and 'pussy cat' show the close relationship between Susan's spoken language and her reading. She has not completely mastered the one to one matching of spoken and printed words, and the addition or omission of one word in the text does not yet concern her.

Figure 6 Example of running record

Susan has been at school for almost a term. She is reading from one of the early Ready to Read books at the red level. Words read correctly are recorded with a tick; repetitions, self-corrections and substitutions are noted. At the conclusion of the passage her accuracy score and self-correction rates are calculated. Accuracy rates are an indication of the degree of difficulty the book poses for the reader. Below 90 per cent is usually considered too difficult for the child; between 90 per cent and 95 per cent is considered a suitable level of difficulty for instructional reading and an accuracy level of above 95 per cent suggests that the book is suitable for the child to read independently. Of equal importance to the statistical calculations are the teacher's interpretation of what the figures mean and the teacher's interpretation is given after the statistics have been worked out.

Informal reading inventories (IRIs)

These typically consist of a standardised series of graded passages of text, which individual children read aloud to the teacher, and then respond to open-ended comprehension questions. The teacher will normally count oral reading errors (accuracy), self-correction, and the number of comprehension questions answered correctly. Sometimes the speed or rate of reading is also assessed. Administration time is typically twenty to thirty minutes per child. Many IRIs have norms to indicate reading ages. Widely used IRIs in New Zealand include the following:

1 **Holdaway's Informal Prose Inventory** (Ashton Scholastic, 1972)
   Consists of nine graded passages, covering five to fourteen years. Tests accuracy, comprehension, rate, word attack, structural analysis, sight vocabulary. No norms or reliability estimates are provided.

2 **Neale Analysis of Reading Ability** (Revised, ACER, 1988)
   Two equivalent forms (1 and 2). Tests accuracy, comprehension and rate of reading. Provides 'Reading Ages' six to twelve years, based on Australian norms. Provides for analysis of errors in reading. Highly reliable test scores. Supplementary tests of letters, sounds and spelling available.

3 **Wellington Departmental Prose Inventory** (1984)
   Consists of two reading passages graded for each half-year level from five to eight-and-a-half years, and for each year level from nine to sixteen years (twenty-four passages). The teacher records errors, self-corrections, whether meaning is maintained and comprehension level. The child moves up a level if reading with 95 per cent accuracy. Prepared by Wellington Reading Advisers.

4 **LARIC Passages** (1983)
   These are graded passages, ranging from five to fourteen years. Teachers record child's miscues, and self-corrections and classify miscues according to cues used. Child may also be required to retell the story. The passages were not originally intended for formal testing or age level placement. Prepared by developers of LARIC (Later Reading In-Service Course).

These various inventories have been widely used by teachers for their *diagnostic value*. Research on the reliability of their use for *age level placements* shows that they are not well suited for this particular purpose (McKenna, 1983). The use of only one or two passages at each age level is often insufficient, especially when the questions vary in difficulty. Moreover, it is not good practice to test children's rate or comprehension from an oral reading 'performance', as some children are more concerned with their delivery under those circumstances than they are when reading silently. Thus, attention to meaning and speed of reading may fluctuate unpredictably and uncharacteristically.

Nevertheless, for informal purposes — to observe children's reading behaviour, and to gain insight into their strategies — using a kind of standardised interview, IRIs share the same advantages as running records, and have potential to reveal more, provided their limitations of reliability are kept in mind.

Tests of word recognition

For some purposes teachers may like to use one of a number of word recognition tests. These consist of a list of isolated words, selected for their frequency of occurrence in children's books, and graded for difficulty. Children read the words aloud and are marked for correct pronunciation. Although such tests measure only a limited aspect of the reading process, they may be useful as a first screen, in clarifying a child's current grasp of word recognition skills, providing an age equivalent level, and sometimes for showing a child's word attack strategies.

The **Burt Word Reading Test** (Gilmore et al, NZCER, 1981) has been revised and normed on New Zealand children (ie, it can indicate the equivalent word reading levels for New Zealand children aged between six and twelve years eleven months.) It consists of 110 isolated words to be read aloud. It is administered individually, takes only a few minutes to give, and shows relatively high reliability for the small sample of words given. Though popular with teachers, the test has many critics (eg, Harrison, 1991) and its limited validity should be kept in mind. It does not measure a child's comprehension, vocabulary range, or use of context and correlates only moderately well with tests of such important factors, especially after children develop beyond the early stages.

For five- and six-year-olds Dr Marie Clay's **Word Tests** are widely used, and form part of the Diagnostic Survey (or 'Six Year Net'), described below.

Several other word recognition tests like the Burt have been developed (eg, Schonell, Fieldhouse) but for most, the norms are outdated and the selection of words probably inappropriate today.

Tests of silent reading comprehension

For more formal testing of children's ability to draw meaning from continuous text — the prime purpose of reading — reliable and standardised tests are available. Some schools have invested time and effort in preparing such tests, often with excellent outcomes. However, it is not easy to produce tests with acceptable reliability and an adequate range of text types and topics to avoid the problem of bias due to culture or specific knowledge. Children read best on topics they are interested in and knowledgeable about (Marr & Gormley, 1982), so that a short test, which includes only two or three passages, may not do justice for all pupils.

Typical test formats (after about Standard 1), require children to read graded passages (silently), and then to respond to written questions on what they have read. The questions may be open-ended, or multiple-choice. They may ask students for main points, to follow directions, to note sequences or to make inferences about the characters, the plot, the author's views, preceding events, and the like. The passages may range in length from fifty words to 1500 words. They should normally be self-contained, interesting, authentic, and cover a range of topics and genres — narrative, expository, persuasive. Sometimes a cloze procedure is used, where the pupils are asked to read texts with every (say) fifth word omitted, and to fill the blanks with the missing words — which they infer from context. Misspellings are ignored. Good readers (from about Standard 2 and upwards) can do this task well, and cloze test results are found to correlate highly with traditional comprehension test results on the same material (Bormuth, 1969; Elley, 1984). Such tests can be modified to test particular words or parts of speech, and can help with diagnosis, especially with ESL children.

Commonly used reading comprehension tests in New Zealand schools include the following:

1 **Progressive Achievement Tests (PAT) of Reading Comprehension**
   (Reid & Elley, NZCER, 1969, Revised 1991)
   Designed for use in Standard 2 to Form 4. Two parallel forms. Eight passages and 40+ multiple-choice questions for each class level. Provides New Zealand percentile rank norms, by class and age. Also provides criterion-referenced levels, to help match pupils with materials. Articulated with Listening Comprehension Tests to help identify children achieving below expectation. Reliability close to 0.90 on each form.

2 **GAP Reading Comprehension Tests** (J McLeod, Heinemann 1965 – 67)
   Cloze test designed for use in Australian primary schools (age seven to twelve years). Two parallel forms (B and R). Seven short graded passages and forty-two blanks to be filled in, in fifteen minutes. Provides reading ages based on Australian norms, for seven to twelve years, but not accurate above ten years. Reliability of each form about 0.83.

3 **GAPADOL Reading Comprehension Tests** (J McLeod & J Anderson, Heinemann, 1972)
   Cloze test designed for use in Australian secondary schools. Two parallel forms (G and Y). Six graded passages and 80+ blanks to be filled in. Provides reading ages based on Australian norms from seven-and-a-half years to sixteen years and ten months. Reliability of each form about 0.85.

Tests of vocabulary

One of the most reliable indicators of reading ability is provided by a simple test of vocabulary, or word knowledge. Children who know the meanings of many words, presented in appropriate contexts, show that they have read widely and learned to infer the meanings of many words from the context. (Nagy et al,1985; Elley, 1989)

Vocabulary knowledge correlates highly with many other kinds of reading ability. For summative testing they are quick, efficient and they account for most of the variance in researchers' attempts to understand the nature of reading comprehension. However, they are less helpful for diagnosis.

In New Zealand classrooms the most commonly used tests are the **Progressive Achievement Test of Reading Vocabulary** (Reid & Elley, 1991). Like the reading comprehension tests, they are designed for children in Standard 2 to Form 4, they come in two parallel forms, they provide percentile rank norms by class and age, and they also give a criterion-referenced estimate of the number of words for which children know meanings.

In Clay's Diagnostic Survey for six-year-olds (Clay, 1985) a **Writing Vocabulary** test is used to show how many words the child knows. This test has been found to correlate well with other reading scores. Breadth of vocabulary can be assessed informally, too, by counting the number of words children use (in their writing or speech) which are not included in common word lists (eg, Spell-Write, NZCER, 1982; Arvidson, 1960; Elley et al, 1979). These assessments measure the child's *active* vocabulary, which is smaller than their *recognition* vocabulary, assessed by a reading vocabulary test.

Diagnostic Survey for five–six-year-olds (the 'six year net')

Dr Marie Clay developed the tests of the Diagnostic Survey (Clay, 1985) particularly for children in the first year of school. It is now used officially as a selection measure for the Reading Recovery programme (on the child's sixth birthday) and at the point of discontinuation from that programme.

Although the tests do have norms to help interpretation, they were designed primarily for diagnosis and criterion-referenced assessment. Details of the contents and administration of the six components of the survey are given in Clay's manual (1985). The six component tests are:

1   **Letter identification**. Children read the letters of the alphabet in upper and lower case. Provides stanine norms (9 to 1).

2   **Word test**. Children read aloud fifteen words selected from the Ready to Read booklets. Three parallel forms (A, B, C). Provides stanine norms (9 to 1).

3   **Concepts about print**. Test of understanding of book conventions — (eg, front, back, word, letter, full-stop, direction, etc). These are important

prerequisite concepts in learning to read. Contains twenty-four items, based on a specially-constructed booklet. Two parallel forms. Provides stanine norms (9 to 1).

4   **Writing vocabulary**. Children write down as many words as they can think of in ten minutes. Child is prompted if production ceases. Useful index of development over time. Highly correlated with reading ability. Provides stanine norms (9 to 1).

5   **Dictation test**. Children write one of a set of five simple sentences read aloud by the teacher. Given credit for each correct phoneme. Provides stanine norms (9 to l).

6   **Running record**. Children read aloud from three book selections (easy text, instructional text and hard text) while teacher records correct and incorrect responses. Follow up analyses show accuracy rates, self-corrections, and cue systems the child is using. The book which is read with 95 per cent accuracy is recorded as the current (instructional) book level.

Volume of reading

A successful reading programme should increase the volume of reading children do. So a teacher will sometimes seek an index of the amount of reading done by her children. This could be achieved by methods such as the following:

1   Counting their library books borrowed.

2   Asking them to list all books read in a given time period.

3   Encouraging them to keep a diary of their leisure activities.

4   Constructing an Author Recognition Test and/or a Title Recognition Test and asking pupils to tick those they know. The inclusion of fictitious names (foils) helps make such measures more reliable. (Stanovich, 1990)

Attitudes to reading

One important aim of reading programmes is to create in children a positive attitude towards reading, to hook them on to books. This can be attempted by regular observation or by using attitude scales. These can take several forms. For example:

1   **Ranking of subjects**

One simple procedure is to ask children to rank in order of their preference the subjects they study at school (Maths, Art, Reading, Science...) in order to determine how popular reading is in relation to other school curriculum areas. New Zealand large-scale surveys show that girls typically rate it high (second after Art) while boys place it about third or fourth. (Elley, 1985)

2   **Ranking of leisure activities**

Children can be asked to rank reading in relation to other leisure time activities, such as television, listening to music, playing computer games, going to movies, playing outdoor sports, etc. In relation to these popular activities, reading may not fare so well.

3   **Likert Attitude Scale**

In a Likert scale, children are asked to agree or disagree (on a 5 point scale) with a series of opinions about reading. Typical statements might be:

	Strongly agree	Agree	Not sure	Disagree	Strongly disagree
1 I feel happy when I'm reading	5	4	3	2	1
2 I only like books with lots of pictures	5	4	3	2	1
3 Books are mostly full of dull stories	5	4	3	2	1
4 I like to read some stories over and over again	5	4	3	2	1

For younger children, the scale could be reduced to three, or even two levels of agreement, and they could respond with tick, question-mark, cross, or by checking a smiling or frowning cartoon face. For positive statements, the score increases by 5 for each 'strongly agree' choice, by 4 with each 'agree' choice, etc. For negative statements the scores are reversed. Such scales give a quantitative index which *can* be reliable, if children are honest, consistent and insightful in their responses. For assessing the average of a total class or group, anonymity can be an advantage in encouraging honesty.

Study Skills

Children are expected to learn to study independently, to consult encyclopedias and dictionaries, to skim for information, to find their way around library catalogues, to recognise when they have identified relevant information, and the like. Much can be learned by regular observation, but a more thorough analysis of the strengths and weaknesses of a class can be obtained fairly quickly with a group test of such study skills. Some teachers do assess these skills with teacher-made tests. However, a series of standardised tests of study skills has been developed by NZCER, with national norms to show how pupils of any class (between Standard 3 and Form 5) compared with a cross-section of children at the same class or age level.

The **PAT Study Skills Tests** (Reid et al, 1978) consist of three separate tests:

1 *Knowledge and use of reference materials*: includes tests of student ability in using dictionaries, lists, encyclopedias, library catalogues and other references.

2 *Reading maps, graphs, tables and diagrams*: includes tests of student ability to interpret maps, several types of graphs, many types of tables and charts, cartoons, and illustrations.

3 *Reading study skills*: includes tests of skimming skills, recognising relevant material, distinguishing fact from opinion, outlining and summarising.

The tests can show teachers when discrepancies exist between their pupils' skills and those of other children at similar stages of development, and indicate where extra emphasis is required. Croft (1984) has provided a useful addition to the Teachers Manual on how best to use the test results for diagnostic purposes. The list of study skills provided in the Manual is also a very useful checklist for teachers.

Summary

This chapter has outlined a number of purposes for assessing children's reading, and shown that different assessment techniques are needed to serve these purposes appropriately. The tests described vary in their reliability and in their validity in different contexts, so that teachers need to be aware of the strengths and limitations of each technique. No reading test is perfect.

It is important to remember also, that testing is undertaken to help children improve. It is not an end in itself. Effort should not stop when the results are recorded. If the results are not used to help the children enhance their comprehension, or to choose their books more carefully, or for some other competency, then the time spent on assessment has been wasted.

Chapter 10

How well do our children read?

Every few years there is an upsurge in criticism of the 'standards' of reading in our schools. Employers, editors, politicians, academics, and indeed many parents express their concern that children are not reading 'as well as they used to', that literacy levels are declining, or that schools spend too little time on basic reading skills.

It is right and proper that the community should be concerned about the achievement levels of the next generation. Indeed, every community appears to do likewise. Criticism of the standards of children's literacy can be found in newspapers and annual reports of the education authorities in all western countries, and in all eras. It seems that there never has been a golden age, when all were reading intelligently and writing fluently.

For instance, in the *Christchurch Press* editorial of 22 May 1916, the editor complained that 'there must be something deplorably wrong when pupils from the primary schools on passing to the secondary schools are found wanting in a working knowledge of the elements of English.'

In the *Listener* of 15 September 1944, the Professor of History at Auckland University was quoted as saying that a quarter of his Stage I students were illiterate — that 'they had not been taught to read accurately and profitably'.

In 1951 the Annual Conference of the Chambers of Commerce urged the Education Department to take action because of their 'inescapable conclusion that by far the majority of pupils of both primary and secondary stages fall very short in their knowledge of the three R's, and the English language'.

Similar claims are made in the 1990s. In an article for *North & South* (June 1993) Jenny Chamberlain argued that 'New Zealand's illiteracy is a huge national problem bubbling away under the lid of our complacency.' Meanwhile, the Minister of Information Technology in the United Kingdom claimed publically that British schools are 'turning out dangerously high quotas of illiterate unemployables', while Jonathan Kozol (1985) estimated that 30 per cent of the American population were not able to read their daily newspapers. Similar complaints are common in Australia and Canada.

Of course, most of these claims are based on personal impressions, on a limited number of anecdotes. They are frequently made by well educated critics, whose regular preoccupations revolve around the use of words, who enjoy daily practice at meaningful reading and writing, and who have forgotten (or never knew) how they and their school mates struggled with the challenging tasks of literacy. The truth is that many children in all generations never learned to read or write. However, their problems were scarcely noticed in a society where there were many manual jobs for the less literate. Now that such work opportunities are on the wane, it is more urgent that the percentage of non-readers be kept to an absolute minimum; that everyone master the arts of reading and writing, as they are key generic skills, which so often determine how far children will proceed with their education, how well they will adapt to changing job requirements, and how well they will be able to educate themselves and their own children. We cannot ignore, then, the protests of those who see inadequacies, even if their charges are based on inadequate evidence. If any child leaves school unable to read or write, there is cause for self-examination.

Nevertheless, the best evidence we have presents quite a different picture from that portrayed by the protestors that so easily gain media attention. New Zealand children are excellent readers by international standards. Cross-national surveys of reading achievement, using fair tests, administered under standardised conditions, to large representative cross-sections of children, of comparable age, in many countries, have consistently shown that New Zealand achievement levels in reading are very high. This evidence is examined below.

Furthermore, expert commentators from other countries have been fulsome in their praise for our reading programmes, our reading teachers, our reading materials and our Reading Recovery methods. New Zealand has a large number of world-renowned children's authors; the Ready to Read series of readers in the junior school is very popular in New Zealand and overseas; our school and public libraries are well stocked with a rich array of good literature; our methods of teaching — shared reading, language experience, regular silent reading, story reading and telling to children, frequent book discussions and displays — all these methods are spreading to other parts of the world. And the Reading Recovery method, developed by Dr Marie Clay in Auckland, has been exported to, and is firmly entrenched in, Australia, the United States, Canada and the United Kingdom. It is no wonder that New Zealand is held up as the country whose reading programmes are 'best in the world' (*Newsweek*, 1992).

What is the evidence on New Zealand reading standards?

Some visitors to New Zealand have visited a range of schools, studied our reading materials, observed teachers and pupils at work, and have expressed their admiration to educators and friends back home. Some have written extensively and enthusiastically about what they saw (eg, Ellen Silverman, *US Teacher*, April 1993; Arthur Goodfriend, *Listener*, 6 June, 1987). However fulsome their praise, it can be argued that they may have seen a biased sample of schools, or that the children they observed were enjoying themselves, but not necessarily learning effectively.

One stronger source of evidence is provided by the cross-national surveys of the International Association of the Evaluation of Educational Achievement (IEA). This is a federation of educators from fifty or more countries, who meet in an Annual Assembly, to plan and conduct surveys of teaching and learning of the students in their schools. In 1970–1 fifteen countries, including New Zealand, took part in an IEA comparative study of reading comprehension (Thorndike, 1973). Ten countries also took part in another survey of literature interpretation and comprehension (Purves, 1973).

In the reading survey, representatives from the participating countries met frequently, prepared appropriate reading tasks, pilot tested them, and administered them to a cross-section of pupils in each country. Table 3 below shows that New Zealand fourteen-year-old children (Form 4) had the highest mean score of all countries, including the United States, England, Scotland, Sweden, Australia — all countries with which we like to compare ourselves. (Australia did not participate in the 1970 survey, but used the same tests in a later study: Bourke and Keeves, 1976) This table shows the actual mean scores for the national samples, while the second column gives the corresponding results for the Form 7 group. Once again, New Zealand pupils had the highest average scores. However, this comparison is less defensible, as the proportion of students who stayed on to Form 7 was lower in New Zealand than in most other countries. New Zealand children were clearly outstanding in their reading comprehension at both levels, but the weaker readers may not have been included in the survey of the older age group.

	Mean scores	
	Pop IV (14 yrs)	Pop IV (17–18 yrs)
New Zealand	29.3	35.4
Italy	27.9	23.9
USA	27.5	21.8
Belgium (France)	27.2	27.6
Finland	27.1	30.0
Scotland	27.0	34.4
Sweden	25.6	26.8
Hungary	25.5	23.8
(Australia)	25.3	
Netherlands	25.3	31.2
England	25.3	33.6
Belgium (Flemish)	24.6	25.0
Israel	22.6	25.2
Chile	14.1	16.0
Iran	7.8	4.4
India	5.2	3.5

Table 3 IEA Reading comprehension survey (Thorndike, 1973)

| | Mean scores | |
	Pop II (14 yrs)	Pop IV (17–18 yrs)
New Zealand	24.4	20.6
Finland	22.3	18.7
USA	20.9	17.5
Belgium (France)	19.9	17.5
England	23.0	19.5
Sweden	21.0	18.3
Italy	18.5	18.9
Belgium (Flemish)	17.7	16.4
Chile	12.9	15.7
Iran	5.2	8.9

Table 4 IEA Literature survey (Purves, 1973)

Similar results were found in the surveys of children's literature. At both Form 4 and Form 7 levels, in both literature interpretation and comprehension, New Zealand students had the highest average achievement levels. Our reading and literature programmes may not have been perfect, but they were bringing more students to higher levels of reading comprehension than those of other comparable countries.

These results were obtained in 1970. What has happened since then? The evidence from standardised tests of achievement show that standards changed remarkably little in the next twenty years. Regular checks on the norms of the *Progressive Achievement Tests* (Reid and Elley, 1991) and a comparison of common reading tasks given in both 1968 and 1990, to large national samples, shows virtually no change in students' reading comprehension and vocabulary, at each level from Standard 3 (eight years) to Form 3 (thirteen years). (See Elley, 1993.)

Some would claim that standards of performance should have risen, as expenditure on education increases, book supplies are improved, and teachers are better trained and educated. However, it needs to be pointed out that in New Zealand today nearly 10 per cent of each age group have English as their second language; that most children spend more time watching television and videos than reading out of school (see Elley, 1992); and that the social costs of economic and educational restructuring have left many negative impacts on family and school conditions. These factors were absent in the conditions of 1970.

The IEA survey of 1990–1

The most recent survey of reading-literacy was conducted by IEA in 1990-91 in thirty-two countries at two age levels, nine years (Standard 3) and fourteen years (Form 4). Once again, appropriate reading tasks were prepared by international committees in three areas — *narrative*, *expository* and *documents* (eg, tables, graphs, maps and lists) — and administered to large representative samples of students at each of the two class levels.

Once again, the New Zealand average scores were very high at each age level, but not the highest this time. A study of Figure 7 on page 117 shows that, for fourteen-year-olds (Population B) New Zealand's average score was fourth highest — very similar to second and third — but a little lower than Finland's. New Zealand actually had more students in the top quarter internationally, than any other country. (See Figure 8 on page 117.) However, our students also showed the widest spread of scores. The outstanding abilities of our top quarter were offset by a substantial group of weaker students — students who frequently came from poor and bookless homes, who spoke another language at home, who spent more hours watching TV than they spent at school, and who were often of Maori or Pacific Island origin. There were also many more boys than girls in this group.

The results for Population A (nine-year-olds), showed a similar pattern. Finland produced the highest scores at both age levels: New Zealand children had mean scores a little lower, but similar to those of several European countries, and the United States. It is worth noting that all of these countries spend considerably more on education, per student, than New Zealand.

Many New Zealand children are excellent readers.

Amongst the other major findings, it was revealed that girls achieved at higher levels than boys at age nine, in all countries, but that by age fourteen boys had nearly caught up in expository and documents domains. They were still well behind in comprehending narrative prose, in most countries. New Zealand children showed the second largest gender gap at age nine (favouring girls) and the largest disparity between ESOL and 'mainstream' children at both age levels. There is clearly room for greater effort to improve the reading of our non-English speaking minority groups and particularly those of Polynesian origin.

Another finding should give us pause for thought. Many of the highest-scoring countries begin reading at age seven, while New Zealand was the only country in the top ten that begins formal instruction at age five. Indeed, all the countries where children began formal reading instruction at age five showed large gender gaps at age nine. The boys in each case were struggling, relative to the girls. And the gaps were still large in such countries at age fourteen. There are indications here that many children (especially boys) are not ready for reading at age five, that they cannot rise to adult expectations, and therefore develop negative feelings about reading. We may be spending needless resources on helping them catch up when they may well learn faster at a later age. It is strange that we diagnose so many children as being in need of Reading Recovery twelve months before instruction actually begins in many countries.

Further details and interpretations of this massive survey of 210 000 pupils are contained in an international report by Elley (1992) and in the New Zealand report by Wagemaker (1993).

Summary

Despite regular criticisms of reading standards in our community, the best impartial evidence, from international surveys of achievement, shows that New Zealand pupils are very competent readers, and that we have in fact, consistently produced many outstanding students. Our reading programmes are apparently serving the needs of most of our pupils well, when judged on a common set of sixty to eighty reading tasks which survived the screening process of an international team of reading researchers.

However, there is no room for complacency. Many secondary school students are still weak readers, and they include too many boys, Maoris, Pacific Islanders and children from poor and bookless homes. While many of the problems these students face may be traced to conditions outside the school, it is not enough for educators to turn their backs on them. Without sound literacy skills, their chances of finding fulfilling employment in the world of 21st century are decidedly bleak.

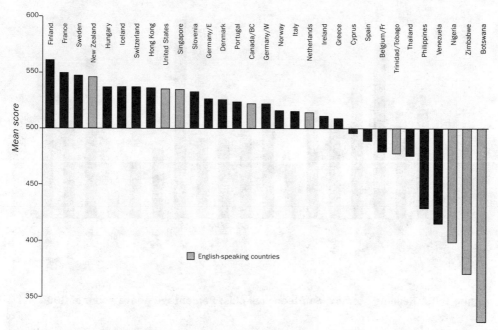

**Figure 7 IEA Reading-literacy: Population B (14 years)
Total achievement scores**

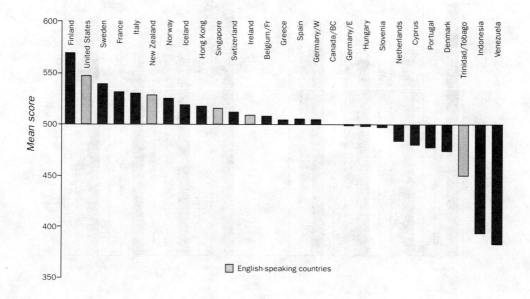

**Figure 8 IEA Reading-literacy: Population A (9 years)
Total achievement scores**

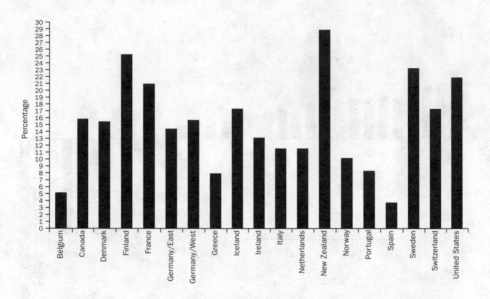

Figure 9 IEA Reading literacy: Fourteen-year-olds: Percentage above score of 600

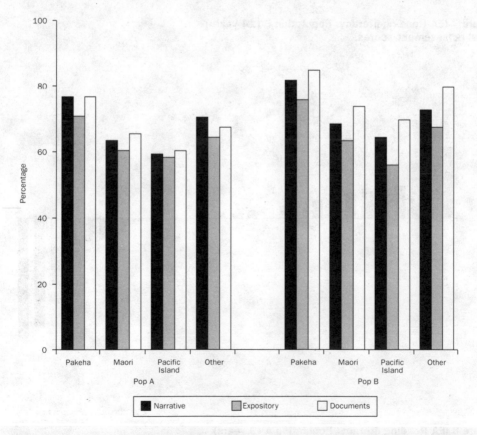

Figure 10 IEA Reading literacy: Mean ethnic differences in reading achievement by domain

Chapter 11

Maori children learning to read

Toi te Kupu
Toi te Mana
Toi to Whenua

The memories that I hold of my very first experiences of reading are very painful and negative. (Moenohotu Plaister, 1993)

...books were things other people had, not us. They were Pakeha things set in a landscape other kids were already accustomed to, the same landscape that was such a nightmare for us. (Witi Ihimaera)

Within the New Zealand education system Maori as a group are consistently underachieving. Compared with Pakeha children, fewer attend preschool. Fewer gain academic qualifications. Fewer pass on to tertiary education. Furthermore, they are over represented in the unemployment statistics and the jail populations and they die younger than Pakeha New Zealanders.

Why should this be so? What relevance does it have to a book about teaching reading? When one group consistently underperforms in an education system the reasons for that must be systemic rather than a result of shortcomings within particular individuals. There is no genetic base for reading. Previous chapters have argued that there are no psychological structures which are unique to reading. Instead, the interplay between political and cultural forces accumulated over many years, has led to Maori being failed by our school system. This pattern of underperformance by an indigenous people is not unique to New Zealand. Australian aborigines, Canadian Inuit and First Nation people, American native people are consistently failed by their education systems.

Ferdman (1990) argues that literacy is a part of cultural identity and should be examined at a group level as well as an individual level. We would include an historical overview in the discussion at a group level.

History

We cannot discuss the present day without some understanding of the past and the history of literacy amongst Maori is particularly illuminating. Jackson

(1979) argues that in the first half of the 19th century Maori enthusiastically adapted European technology and ideas to their existing tribal structure. They grew new crops such as wheat, barley and potatoes; they traded with the settlers and across the Tasman to Australia; they purchased guns from the settlers. Much of the European technology was admired by the Maori, but as Jackson states:

> *Maori people were disinclined to accept the word of the Europeans; they wanted to read the 'word' for themselves and use the advantage of reading and writing in seeking ends they themselves determined. (1979:32)*

In other words Maori saw the written word as giving them access to knowledge which they wanted.

Early missionaries wrote about the speed with which the Maori people acquired literacy. Clark wrote in 1833 :

> *In every village there are several of the natives who can read and write: a school is established among them by the natives themselves, where a number are taught to read and write; old and young are taught their catechism. Their desire for books is very great.*

By 1845 Jackson estimates there was one Maori *New Testament* for every two Maori in New Zealand. Even allowing for missionary hyperbole, in writing back to their superiors in England, the picture is of a whole people enthusiastically acquiring literacy.

The literacy movement started by the missionaries contained its own seeds of destruction. One seed was the decision to teach Maori only in their own language. By restricting literacy instruction to the Maori language (where the only reading material available was the Bible) the missionaries hoped to shield the Maori people from the corrupting influence of 'lewd' literature. This was a paternalistic version of literacy practised by the missionaries. What was important were the books and documents not translated and published in Maori — books and documents dealing with land tenure and title. Letter writing by Maori to the Governor from 1840–1850 showed 'an almost desperate preoccupation with land' (Jackson, 1979:39). But Colenso's printing press only offered more of the scriptures. By 1844 Hatfield noted, with more prescience than he realised at the time:

> *It appears every year more evident that our present system of conveying instruction to these people is wholly inadequate to their present wants; they have been brought to a certain point and we have no means of bringing them beyond that. (quoted by McKenzie, 1985)*

It was not until 1872 that the first book was published to teach Maori to read in English. The main value of literacy to Victorian Maori was for communication between the tribes. The King movement was helped by literacy. Chiefs wrote to each other often about matters of concern. The King movement set up its own newspaper in 1858 (te Hokoi) which led Governor Grey to set up a government newspaper in Te Awamutu in 1862.

Literacy also had a destabilising effect on tribal culture. Replacing an oral tradition with a printed one meant that the memories of traditional tribal experts could be challenged by those who were able to read. Writing gives power and status to those who have the ability to read and write and not, as in oral traditions, to those with the longest and best memories. McKenzie notes that often the people to whom the missionaries taught literacy were slaves and outsiders, people without mana, who congregated around the missions. These people would often go into the country and set up schools to teach the Maori to read — the Bible of course.

Literacy could not help the Maori save the land, nor could it turn back the ever increasing tide of settlers. It did not give them access to the symbols of European power. A time of disillusionment set in and many Maori turned away from literacy, seeking refuge in the symbols and values of the past.

Literacy failed the Maori because the dominant culture introduced it without respect for Maori culture. Perhaps a belief by nineteenth century missionaries in the superiority of European culture is understandable, if not excusable, in its historical context. Today, however, any such beliefs are indefensible. Yet our education system still has not learned the lessons of the nineteenth century and is still failing Maori people.

The situation today

There are many problems which educationists have not come to terms with. For instance, until the arrival of the Europeans, Maori was an oral culture. Today, Maori society values highly the arts of oratory and the oral transmission of culture. The school curriculum, on the other hand, places reading and writing centre stage. This still leads to conflict for many Maori.

Moenohotu (Plaister, 1993) describes growing up in Te Rohe Potae during the 1950s and early sixties, speaking Maori as her first language. She had a close relationship with her mother who took her into the bush gathering plants and taught her myths and legends, as well as local history and place names. At school pride of place was given to book knowledge — information that was written down. Few of us know that Te Rohe Potae is the area the European settlers renamed 'The King Country' in the central North Island. The dominant culture refused to admit the existence of Maori learning, or to give credit to it. In Moe's case this culminated in an argument with a high school teacher who claimed that Maori pa were always built on the tops of hills. The teacher ignored the pa she drove past each morning on the way to school and clung to her belief that pa were only on top of hills 'because the books say so'. There was no place in Moe's school for any books written in Maori, or books in English dealing with Maori themes, or any credence given to the knowledge that an oral culture carries with it.

Identity

If Maori children are to grow up with a stable sense of identity, it is important that reading materials show a range of people involved in many different activities. This has not been the case with Maori. Beaglehole (1982) surveyed Maori content in School Journals from 1907 to 1981, at five yearly intervals. Overall, 5 per cent of the content related to Maori culture or language. Within that 5 per cent was a swing away from the journals of early years, which had portrayed Maori as noble savages and victorious warriors living in a glorious past, to more modern day journals which portrayed contemporary Maori life, albeit as rural rather than urban dwellers. However, while stories featuring Maori average only 5 per cent of the content of Beaglehole's study, the proportion of adult Maori in New Zealand has increased to over 12 per cent and the proportion of children to 20 per cent. In a more recent study, Caddick (1992) surveyed School Journals in 1979, and 1987–1990, to determine ethnic and cultural representation. She found that Maori character representation in School Journals had changed little from the 5 per cent Beaglehole found in 1982, to 6 per cent in 1992. Caddick comments:

> Non-Pakeha were underrepresented in positions of authority, power and social recognition... over one third of the activities in which Maori are represented involved food in some way. (1992:23)

The stories and books we place before our pupils need to represent accurately the characters they are attempting to portray. The 1962 Ready to Read series had Maori characters but the only way they represented Maori was in their names. Their appearance, their actions, their language, was that of Pakeha with a good suntan.

Moenohotu describes the reactions of her mother and herself to the readers she brought home from school:

> Notes were sent home to my mother to encourage her to read to me, books were sent home with me as well. An example: Nursery Rhyme..Jack and Jill went up the hill to fetch a pail of water. I spent a lot of time giggling. The book had one word, the English had another word, the Maori had another word, but nothing looked like the white enamel bucket that my brother used when he went down the hill to fetch our water from the spring. (Plaister, 1993)

Ihimaera describes how the reading that his family did at home (*The Weekly News*, *Pix* and Dad's *Best Bets*) was not considered 'real' reading by the school. He and his brothers then did not relate the school version of literacy to the version that was practised at home. He describes the books in the school library as 'things you propped up and yawned behind.'

While we have argued that the restriction of literacy to reading the Bible translated into Maori limited adult Maori's ability to cope with the colonial powers on their terms, the switch for children from education in Maori to education only in English was devastating. Benton (1989:73) describes the experiences of one Maori woman attending school in the 1920s thus:

She had spoken only Maori before going to school, where it was 'beaten out' of her. She used to be punished by being sent up into the bush outside the school, 'and had to spend the rest of the day clearing it away with her bare hands'. She said she did not blame her parents for not teaching their children to speak in Maori 'because they had such a rough time when they were at school'.

Language and culture are inseparable. Forbidding the use of Maori in schools sent a clear message that the culture of the Maori was of little value in a European education system. We are defined by our language. Remove it and there is little left.

Language

Language lies at the heart of learning. The decision by the missionaries to print materials only in the Maori language denied access to Maori on areas of vital interest such as land laws. In the nineteenth century many Maori grew up and lived in Maori speaking communities. The survival of the language appeared certain. Nevertheless, proficiency in English was seen as the key to gaining access to technology, jobs and power.

The Native Schools Act of 1867 specified that teaching and learning be done in English. This Act, along with the 1877 Education Act laid down the legal basis for education. Kaa (1987) states that, as a result of these acts, Maori had no place in the school system 'either as a medium of instruction or a subject' (1987:56).

Today the language situation is reversed. The Maori language is threatened with extinction and Maori are swimming in a sea of English — in the educational institutions, in the media, in the courts and in parliament. Many Maori who are not fluent Maori speakers identify with the Maori language. In spite of the total dominance of the English language, the Waite report (1992) estimates that some 50 000 people have maintained Maori as their first language.

Some disturbing research findings

New Zealand maintains a system of social promotion whereby children are kept with their age mates throughout the eight years of primary school. Geraldine McDonald (1988) examined the promotion of children from junior classes to the standard classes. Her findings were that:

'between a fifth and a quarter of each age cohort (between 10 000 and 12 000 children) are held back every year at the point at which they move from the junior classes to the standard classes...within this large group of retained children there are enduring differentials. Non-Maori girls have the greatest chance of being promoted, then non-Maori boys have somewhat less chance, then Maori girls and finally Maori boys. Thirty per cent of Maori boys are kept back.' (1991:2)

Retaining children for another year in the junior classes may be justified if there is a rational basis for keeping the child in the junior classes but McDonald's work suggests there is not. McDonald considers that the determining factor in decisions about promotion is 'not in the children themselves and their ability, but in the ideas held by the teachers who determine promotion.' (1991:4)

Junior class interactions

Marie Clay(1985) and Courtney Cazden(1988) have carried out observational studies on who gets attention from the teacher. Clay and her assistants spent six mornings a week in terms one and two in six Auckland new entrant classrooms observing teacher-child interactions. The observations were focused on how teachers provided for cultural differences in the classroom. Six target children were observed in each classroom — two Maori, two Pakeha and two Pacific Island children.

The results show firstly a remarkable degree of on-task behaviour — more than 90 per cent of the time the children were on task and there were no significant ethnic differences in this high rate of engagement. Clay noted that 'Data on attention to teacher, and attention to seat-work tasks showed that most children were on task more than 90 per cent of the time.' (1985) Apparently the reading programmes held the children's attention well.

There was also a high rate of individual teacher-child interactions. Clay commented that: 'It was possible to locate many episodes where a teacher sat alongside a child and did some teaching...It was usual to obtain five or six episodes of teacher-child interaction for each child on each of five or six observation mornings.' (1985:28–30) The disturbing aspect of this study is that teacher's interactions varied according to the ethnicity of the child. Clay coded her observations into a number of categories including a 'talk more' category. This category encourages children to elaborate on their previous utterances. Cazden (1988) summarised Clay's work in these terms:

> During Clay's observations in the first term teachers asked European and Pacific Island children to talk more about whatever was the topic of conversation more than five times per morning but made the same request of the Maori children less than four times. (1988:10)

While such differences may appear small (one less 'talk more') each day, if they are added up for two years, then it becomes obvious that children from one ethnic group are receiving significantly less attention from the teacher than their peers. Does this matter? In a word — yes. Brief reference was made in previous chapters to the work of Vygotsky. If learning can be best facilitated by social interaction using language, then a group of children are being denied the opportunity to make progress comparable to their peers.

Clay's findings do not mean that teachers are consciously discriminating against one particular group in the classroom. The teachers were not aware that they were responding differently to one group in their classroom. The teachers considered that they were following an established pattern for successful teaching by moving around their class and interacting individually with children. Cazden, in attempting to tease out the implications of Clay's findings, suggests that perhaps there is too much emphasis on junior class teachers working individually with children. Cazden suggests that:

> *It may be helpful to differentiate between individualism as a way of organising a learning environment and personalisation as a quality of the interactions in that environment, however it is organised. It seems possible to this foreign observer that the ideal of individualisation may be more a part of Pakeha culture than an essential part of successful junior classrooms for Maori children.(1988:20)*

What should be done?

Ferdman's (1990) comments about literacy being a matter of cultural identity provide a theoretical base from which to argue that ways to enhance the literacy of Maori need to be implemented from a broad base which recognises the role society plays in constructing literacy. The solutions are not spectacular and have been asked for by Maori educators, such as Ranganui Walker, Smith and Jenkins, for many years. We need more Maori teachers in school, more Pakeha teachers who can speak Maori and more materials which reflect contemporary Maori culture and aspirations. Above all we must listen to the Maori people and work harder to support their efforts in education. Kohanga

Children sharing a suitable book with their teacher.

reo is producing a new generation of Maori speaking children. But too often they move to a monoglot English-speaking primary school, and their language is submerged again. Maori parents will no longer allow a Pakeha school system to ignore the tangata whenua.

There are encouraging signs of progress. Learning Media puts a quarter of its annual funding into Maori language publications (Waite, 1992:41). The number of books written in Maori published by Learning Media has increased and the 1993 catalogue lists thirty books written in Maori and sixteen audio tapes. In 1988 there were twenty bilingual primary schools in New Zealand, and sixty-seven primary schools with bilingual classes. The first Kura Kaupapa Maori was established in 1987 at the Hoani Waititi Marae and five others became state schools in 1989. But in themselves these measures are not enough.

We must examine the reasons for literacy failure at a societal level. Poor housing, poor nutrition, lack of individual recognition of a culture, combine to slow progress at school. The solution is not to berate individuals but to identify the barriers to progress and remove them.

Maori-medium primary schools

The Waite report (1992) considers that the best way to provide for the long term survival of the Maori language is to have schools where the medium of instruction for all subjects is Maori. Waite cites research conducted in the Basque country in Spain showing that children whose daily school instruction was in Basque scored at a higher level in tests of the Basque language than children in bilingual programmes, who in turn scored more highly than those children in Spanish-medium programmes. Interestingly, in Spanish language tests, there was no difference between the three groups despite the children in the Basque-medium programmes having less teaching in Spanish that those in the Spanish language programmes.

There are problems with providing schools where the medium of instruction is Maori. One is the shortage of qualified Maori-speaking teachers. Another is the scarcity of materials written in the Maori language. Both of these issues are gradually being overcome. Moreover, the School of Education at Waikato University and the Auckland College of Education now offer teacher education courses in the Maori language.

What teaching strategies should be used?

If the Maori language is accorded its rightful status as an official language of New Zealand in schools and there is a continuing rise in the availability of books in the Maori language, there is no need to change the teaching methods advocated throughout this book. Research conducted internationally has shown that whole language techniques are effective regardless of the language of instruction. Elley (1991) reviewed nine studies in predominantly Pacific countries where children were taught to read in English (their second language) by whole language techniques. These studies were contrasted with progress made by children learning to read in English through programmes based on 'structured systematic instruction'. Elley (1991) concludes that:

> the effects of programmes that expose young children to large quantities of high-interest illustrated story books have shown that rapid improvement occurs in reading and listening comprehension, and that gains transfer readily to all aspects of the pupil's target language. The effects are stable, and occur in pleasant, non-threatening contexts, with associated gains in attitudes towards reading and books. (1991:108)

It is too early to assess the impact of Maori-language schools on the literacy progress of young Maori children. Early anecdotal reports are encouraging however, and there is good reason to believe that the phonetic regularity of the Maori language may present fewer hurdles for young readers in the early stages than English does, with its many phonetic inconsistencies.

Chapter 12

Helping children with reading difficulties

So far we have described the pattern of class teaching, and its research base, as it applies to children making steady progress through the school system. Our attention now turns to children who are not progressing satisfactorily.

This chapter will address the problems of definition and of the numbers of children involved. The chapter concludes with a detailed description of two successful New Zealand programmes to alleviate reading failure.

How can we define reading difficulty?

This is an area fraught with difficulties. There is no terminology which is universally accepted by teachers, parent groups or psychologists. The Department of Education (1972) used to distinguish between 'backward readers' and 'retarded readers'. The difference between the two groups was alleged to be that backward readers were reading below average for their age or class, while retarded readers were reading below what was expected, considering their general ability or intelligence.

Today our vocabulary, if not our knowledge, has widened and children who are having difficulty with literacy at school are showered with a wide and impressive sounding number of labels ranging from 'learning disabled' to 'brain damaged' and including, along the way, 'dyslexia,' 'minimal brain dysfunction,' 'neurological impairment' — the list goes on. What remains constant is not the label, or the hypothesised explanation, but the fact that some children do experience difficulty with learning to read and that there are no simple solutions to their difficulties. Children who do not make satisfactory progress may have visual or auditory difficulties; they may come from bookless homes and see no point or purpose in reading; they may be unhappy children, with emotional blocks which interfere with their concentration; they may have been absent from school at critical stages; or they may have been badly taught. It is also possible that they may have been pushed into formal instruction before they were ready. Children in Scandinavia postpone reading instruction until age seven, yet they become very good readers. (Elley, 1992)

Problems of definition

Why is it so difficult to define the concept of reading difficulties? One problem is that the categories contained in the definition can also be applied to children who are making satisfactory progress in reading. For example, some children with 'brain damage' appear to learn to read quite well. Also, if a backward reader is reading below average for the class, one should ask how the class average is worked out. Every class has a wide range of achievement levels and the average changes according to the tests used. Indeed, any working out of a mythical class average may well be based on inadequate assessment procedures, such as a word recognition test or an informal reading inventory too short to be reliable.

Similarly, with reading expectancy, how is one to establish a child's expected level of achievement? Expectancy formulae usually involve some form of 'intelligence tests...together with informal observations and available records.' (See *Reading Suggestions for Teaching Reading in Primary and Secondary Schools*.) If a child's reading age is measured as two years below his/her mental age, as determined by an intelligence test, then the child is said to be retarded. Work by Ballard (1980), however, suggests that the whole concept of intelligence has little relevance here. An intelligence test is itself a measure of achievement, and usually requires the child to read. It is not therefore an adequate test of how well a child might be able to read under ideal conditions. It is not a test of genetic potential. Also, even if the notion of a 'reading expectancy' is accepted, there are ethical problems to consider, particularly when allocating scarce resources. Some argue that children who are of average intelligence, or above, and are failing in reading for no apparent sensory or socio-cultural reasons, are 'learning disabled'. Does this definition mean that children who score at the lower levels of intelligence tests cannot be learning disabled and should not be given assistance with reading? It seems grossly unfair to provide help only to those children who score at the average and upper levels in intelligence tests. We face a dilemma when considering reading potential as a criterion by which assistance is offered or withheld from children. As Vernon (cited by Clay, 1987) stated:

> *Neither genetic potential nor constitutional potential are of any use to us for predicting likely achievement since we cannot measure them.*

Terms such as dyslexia, and learning disability are widely used, but have never been adequately defined. The dictionary definition of dyslexia is 'word blindness' and many people assume it implies some kind of brain impairment, and is characterised by reversals. The child reads 'b' for 'd' or 'was' for 'saw'. But many normal children make such reversals when learning to read. Also a neurological impairment which is specific only to reading does not exist — if significant neurological impairment is present, as for example in people who have cerebral palsy, the entire range of language processes as well as others are affected. Perhaps dyslexia is a term that correlates highly with parent income and status — an unemployed carpenter has a child who 'has difficulty reading' whereas a wealthy lawyer's child who has similar difficulties is labelled 'dyslexic.'

In an important article discussing the concept of learning disabilities, Clay (1987) contends that the term is impossible to define clearly. She considers that there is no valid way to distinguish between low achieving readers and learning disabled children. She argues that children learn to become 'learning disabled' (which she uses as the title of her paper) by learning and practising an inappropriate set of responses to instruction. Instead of arguing as to whether a response is the result of inappropriate learning or organic brain damage, researchers and teachers should be trying to find ways to observe the child's responses and find ways of changing inappropriate responses. Remediation is most effective, according to Clay, when it is based on an understanding of the way fluent readers read, rather than a futile attempt to diagnose organic brain defects.

Clay (1987) sums up an extensive review of the literature relating to learning disabilities:

> *The Learning Disability concept which seemed to hold so much promise in the 1960s has been espoused by legal, medical, psychological and educational professionals but research and analysis has not produced a useful definition, effective identification or discriminated this condition from other similar states by etiology, diagnosis, treatment or prognosis. The wide use of such an ill-defined category implies that children are being classified as Learning Disabled when there is no agreement on how they should be helped, scant evidence of programmes that work, and little effort to find such programmes. (1987:170)*

We suggest that for the classroom teacher, as well as for the researcher, the pursuit of psychological or neurological defects as a way of explaining reading failure is largely a waste of time. Rather than labelling we need to be developing teaching strategies that will help all children learn to read successfully. If some form of definition is required (for whatever purposes) then a simple one is most effective. We consider that a remedial reader is a person who has passed the emergent reading stage but still requires some assistance with reading. They cannot read what they need to read. This definition avoids fruitless excursions into arcane psychological theorising. It is a definition which can also be applied to people of all ages. When confronted with a legal document, most of us become remedial readers and seek the help of a more skilled reader. In the case of legal documents, many lawyers have become rich through their ability to read, and sometimes to explain to their clients, legal documents whose readability is unnecessarily obtuse. This is no different from a child who, confronted with a difficult text, asks the teacher or a peer what the story is about. Clay (1987) comments:

> *I do not need an elaborate definition of reading difficulties. One simply takes the pupil — child, adolescent or adult — from where he is to somewhere else. There is not one of us who could not read better if we had individual instruction in reading now. (1987:55)*

An alternative approach to categorising children by some abstract notion of disability is to see how many children in New Zealand are having difficulty with reading and are receiving regular extra help.

How many children receive extra help?

The Ministry of Education Research and Data Management Analysis Bulletin (May 1993) reports that in 1992 approximately 14 235 children took part in Reading Recovery (1993:40) and that 1 888 children were enrolled in programmes taken by Resource Teachers of Reading (1993:46). There are no figures available for the children who were worked with intermittently by teachers or for those children involved in peer or parent tutoring programmes. Out of a total primary school population of 421 390, 16 123 children officially received additional help with reading, ie, some 3.8 per cent. These figures are controlled to some extent by the availability of help. The largest group are those children who receive teaching through Reading Recovery which is available to children who are making slow progress at age six. Approximately one child in four, of our six-year-olds, the slowest in their classes, receives such a boost. Reading Recovery will be discussed below. There are also voluntary groups outside the educational establishment such as SPELD (Society for the Prevention and Elimination of Learning Disabilities) who also tutor children who are having difficulty.

Reading Recovery

Reading Recovery is the most well-documented and the most successful reading assistance programme in New Zealand — and possibly the rest of the world. (See Pinnell et al, 1994.) It has a clearly articulated vision of the reading process. The programme grew out of work that Clay began in the 1960s before the publication of her first book, *Reading: The Patterning of a Complex Behaviour* (1972). This book was based on many hours of observing young children's progress in reading in their first year of school. Clay continued her close observations of young children learning to read, and with the collaboration of a group of gifted teachers of young children developed the Reading Recovery Programme in the 1970s.

There are three major threads to Reading Recovery — early identification of children making slow progress, intensive individual instruction with a specially trained teacher, and a return to normal class programmes as soon as possible. Each of these aspects, as well as research evidence about the programmes' efficacy, will be discussed in greater detail below.

Early identification

Clay advocates testing between 30 per cent and 50 per cent of all children at age six. This will have given children a year of instruction at school. If satisfactory progress is not being made after a year, which is sufficient time to allow a child to become settled into school and adjusted to routines, then some alternative form of instruction to class based teaching is needed. In Clay's view, many remedial reading programmes are ineffectual because they are not implemented until the child has experienced failure for a number of years. This is time during which ineffectual strategies have become internalised, and the child has had several years of failure with consequent damage to feelings of self-esteem. Attitudes towards school may have become more negative and a downward cycle of failure begins. Delay in remedial instruction means there is more unlearning of incorrect behaviours required from the child.

Testing children as close to their sixth birthday as possible also allows testing to be spread out over the year and is therefore more convenient logistically.

The diagnostic survey

The survey consists of a number of short tests which are administered individually. Running records of the child's current reading book play an important part. Tests of letter identification, word tests, concepts about print, dictation and a writing test make up the remainder of the survey. All these assessment procedures are based on a careful analysis of the way reading takes place. Rather than look for psychological reasons to account for slow progress, the test battery is designed to help the teacher discover what reading strategies the child possesses and which strategies are lacking. Children's understanding of the concepts about print is tested with a small booklet which looks like many of the books a child is expected to read during a reading programme. Concepts such as directionality, letter and word identification and knowledge of punctuation are tested in the context of this book. There are age norms for the test and results are translated to stanine scores (9 down to 1).

Writing procedures consist of collecting samples of the child's written work and examining them in terms of language, message quality and directionality principles. Writing vocabulary is assessed by simply asking the six-year-old to write down all the words he/she knows — a procedure that is delightfully simple, yet a careful analysis of the results gives an important indicator of a child's understanding of the way print works. A simple dictation test is also part of the survey.

As it is described above, the survey looks like a daunting number of tasks to administer to children but it should be remembered that not all six-year-olds need to be surveyed and for those that do, teaching based on the survey may save many hours of teaching in the future. Early intervention, based on a careful analysis of the child's strengths and weaknesses, is the foundation of Reading Recovery.

Teaching in Reading Recovery

Reading Recovery tutoring is carried out by an experienced teacher who works with children individually for half an hour every day. The basis for teaching is detailed observation, which leads to careful teaching of reading strategies based on the child's needs. Because Reading Recovery children are making slower progress than their age-mates, progress will have to be accelerated if they are to become average progress children. The teacher must keep in mind two kinds of learning:

> *on the one hand there is fluency and performing with success on familiar material and on the other there is a challenge to independent problem-solving in new and interesting texts with supportive teaching. The texts are very carefully selected for the needs of the particular pupil to foster acceleration. (Clay, 1985: 53)*

A description of the actual teaching strategies can be found in *The Early Detection of Reading Difficulties* (3rd edition). Clay argues that the specialised teaching techniques she describes are not required for children making satisfactory progress. Each Reading Recovery session includes reading and writing. It is important that the child recognises the links between reading and writing. Skills are not taught in isolation — rather they are used in the context of reading stories from books. The aim of the teaching is to produce readers who have developed independent reading skills and can self monitor their own progress. It is important that the child does not become dependent on an individual tutor — rather the child must be able as soon as possible to function in the classroom environment and progress at the same rate as his/her peers.

Research evidence

Clay (1985) has described lengthy studies assessing the effectiveness of the Reading Recovery programme. In the initial 1978 study of eighty children in five Auckland schools the children made significant gains in all tests (book level, reading vocabulary, concepts about print, letter identification and dictation) and caught up with the control group of 160 average children in the same schools. One year later the same children were continuing to maintain their trends of progress (1985:95). Three years later a further follow-up study showed that the children were continuing to make progress similar to their age cohort. Clay comments that:

> *As a result of accelerated progress the children typically leave the programme with average levels of performance in three to six months. The success gained with the poorest performers of the group at six years runs counter to the assumptions, expectations and experience in most Western systems. (1985:105)*

The following year the programme was implemented and evaluated in forty-eight schools and the results were just as positive as in the first survey. (Clay, 1985)

Reading Recovery was implemented in Columbus, Ohio in 1985–86 and its progress has been carefully monitored. Pinnell (1989) describes the results:

> *Evidence from the first three years of implementation indicates that Reading Recovery has had positive outcomes for children initially determined to be at risk of failure in reading. Two-thirds or more of children who receive a full program in Reading Recovery make accelerated progress and perform within the average range for their classes. Children retain their gains and continue to make progress at least two years after the intervention. (1989:175)*

The programme has now been implemented in over sixty centres in the United States, often with the help of New Zealand reading specialist tutors.

Wasik and Slavin (1993) reviewed five programmes designed to prevent early reading failure by means of individual tutoring. Reading Recovery was one of the programmes reviewed. Five research studies, carried out in the United States, examining Reading Recovery were studied. The most ambitious study compared three alternative programmes with Reading Recovery as well as a control group in ten Ohio schools. In all studies Reading Recovery children made substantial and sustained gains. With reference to the most ambitious study the authors comment:

> *The effects of Reading Recovery are impressive at the end of the implementation year, and the effects are maintained for at least two years. (1993:187)*

Another glowing report on the comparative effectiveness of Reading Recovery in the US showed that it was more successful than three other models (Pinnell et al, 1994). Similar reports of the success of Reading Recovery come from the United Kingdom. Wright (1993) evaluated the progress of 126 low progress five-and six-year-old children in eleven Surrey schools. After 16.8 weeks of tutoring, on average, 96.4 per cent of the children reached average levels of achievement in reading, and the gains were judged to be equivalent to those reported by Clay in New Zealand. The researchers estimated that the cost per child was approximately £600–800, but that the savings in terms of later unnecessary remedial expenses are much greater than this. Encouraging reports have also come from Australia and Canada, where Reading Recovery has been introduced.

Reading Recovery owes its success to its sound theoretical base, its individual teaching and the intensive training and monitoring of its teachers. It has grown in New Zealand and over one quarter of all six-year-old children receive tuition from the programme. Such children are not necessarily failing, but are 'at risk' and in need of a boost to their progress. New Zealand critics such as Tunmer (1990) have suggested that the time children spend in the programme could be reduced if there was a greater emphasis on building syntactic awareness in a systematic fashion. He has recently demonstrated this assertion with an empirical study (Tunmer, 1992). However, such a criticism misses the point that the programme is an individual one in which observation leads to teaching which suits each child's needs. If a child is seen to need such teaching he/she will get it. Indeed, as Clay points out (1991) the teaching sessions are rich in opportunities for developing the child's syntax.

Other New Zealand critics (Glynn et al, 1989) suggest that the gains made by many children are not sustained and that the programme should be more carefully targeted. It is clear that some schools offer the programme to competent readers, while many other children in schools with major literacy problems, will miss out. Glynn et al also found there were difficulties when children were returned to their normal programme in that classroom teachers often gave children books that were either too easy or too difficult. Continuing progress cannot be guaranteed without competent teaching and regular monitoring.

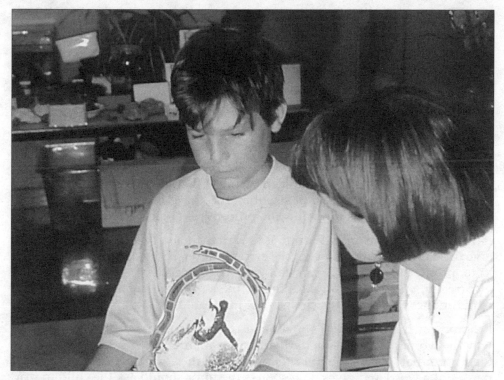

Children benefit from individual help.

We should remember too that Reading Recovery continues to evolve. While the basic principles remain unchanged, details continue to be improved. For example, Clays' early work did not discuss the role that communication between home and school can play to assist children who are at risk of reading failure. These concerns are being addressed now and schools are expected to inform parents when their children are involved in the programme, and of ways they can help their child.

Reading Recovery withdraws children from the classroom for their tuition. Given that the time children spend in the programme is limited and that no more than half an hour a day is spent out of the classroom we do not think that the organisational pattern is counter to the prevailing philosophy of inclusive education.

Finally, the programme is expensive both in time and money. Glynn comments:

> *In all except one of the schools in our sample, and in most other schools that we have knowledge about, Reading Recovery teachers spend 2 to 2.5 hours per day within school hours on teaching, assessment, monitoring and other tasks connected with Reading Recovery. Typically, they include within this time teaching sessions for four children. (1989:133)*

The change in school administration in New Zealand in 1990 has given the schools power over their own finances and it is their decision to budget, or not budget, as they see fit, for Reading Recovery. With the continuing pressure on school budgets it is hoped that when faced with competing demands for a new filter for the swimming pool or new computers, Reading Recovery does not suffer. We should remember that the financial costs of not being able to read remain with a person for their entire life. What price can be put on literacy?

Pause, Prompt and Praise

A totally different remedial programme has been developed by Professor Glynn and his associates over the past fifteen years. Called 'Pause, Prompt and Praise,' this programme uses trained tutors, either parents or peers, to act as tutors. Tutors are given a set of specific procedures to apply to oral reading. Figure 11 on page 137 shows how the procedures are to be applied.

If the child makes an error the tutor is to wait for at least five seconds (pause) to give the child a chance to correct the error; if the error is not corrected the tutor is to prompt the child. Errors fall into two categories — a word is read incorrectly, but the overall meaning of the story is maintained; or the child reads an incorrect word which does not maintain the story meaning.

Prompts can direct the child's attention to either the meaning of the story or the way the word looks and sounds. If after two attempts the reader does not give the appropriate word, the tutor tells the child the correct word. If the reader pauses at a word and gives no response the tutor should ask the child to read again from the beginning of the sentence.

Praise should be given for attempts to correct errors. It is important that praise be specific so the reader knows what is being done correctly. Comments like, 'Well done — that was good reading' offer little in the way of specific feedback to readers. Instead comments such as, 'I like the way you stopped and worked out that word by yourself' are used. Sessions should be no longer than ten minutes and be held at least two or three times weekly.

Pause, Prompt and Praise is not a complete reading programme. It is designed to be used with older children who are experiencing difficulties. Its implementation requires a trained tutor and appropriate texts. Because the programme relies on oral reading it is important that the texts be neither too hard (where the reader makes too many errors and loses the thread of the story) nor too easy (where there are no errors made so no strategies can be reinforced). Glynn suggests that texts where between five and ten errors per one hundred words are made are appropriate.

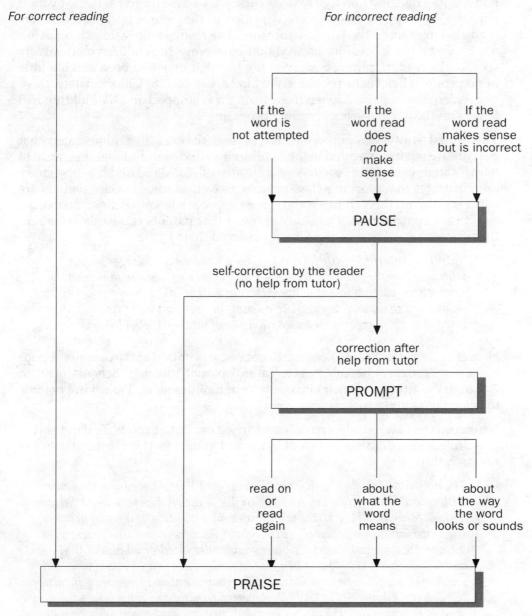

For correct reading

For incorrect reading

If the word is not attempted

If the word read does *not* make sense

If the word read makes sense but is incorrect

PAUSE

self-correction by the reader (no help from tutor)

correction after help from tutor

PROMPT

read on or read again

about what the word means

about the way the word looks or sounds

PRAISE

(*From*, Glynn & Wheldall: 1992)

Figure 11 Pause, Prompt and Praise

Research evidence

The first research study on Pause, Prompt and Praise was carried out in 1978 in the Auckland suburb of Mangere. Fourteen families were studied intensively. Children from these families were aged between eight and twelve years and had reading deficits from two to five years. They were tutored at home by their parents. Appropriate books were supplied to the homes by the researchers who also monitored the parents' tutoring. The results were astonishing. After ten to fifteen weeks, results showed that on average the children made nearly six months reading progress, despite the fact that they had been making little or no progress before the project. (Wheldall & Glynn:118) Unfortunately, these gains were not sustained when the tutoring was stopped and the children had to rely on the normal school reading programme.

This initial study was important for several reasons. It demonstrated that parents are not uninterested in their children's education and that they want to help. Mangere is a lower socio-economic area of Auckland and this first study demonstrates that working class parents as well as middle class parents are concerned about their children and, given appropriate knowledge, can make a significant contribution. The study showed that parents can easily be taught the procedures. Wheldall and Glynn observed that:

> untrained tutoring had little effect on their children's reading. However, following training in these methods and regular feedback sessions from the researchers, parents learnt to delay their attention to children's errors (ie, pause) and to provide appropriate prompts or cues instead of simply telling the word. They also greatly increased their use of praise. (1989:118)

However, as in the case of Reading Recovery, it is important to note that a poor classroom programme can negate careful parent tutoring. Schools need to examine the efficacy of their classroom programmes as well as asking parents to tutor their children.

Numerous research studies have been carried out both in New Zealand and in the United Kingdom since 1978. Glynn and Wheldall (1992) summarise the research thus:

> The majority of studies with Pause Prompt and Praise have involved readers with considerable deficits in reading. In five of the studies reviewed by Glynn and McNaughton (1985), the minimum deficit was two years, and in one study the minimum deficit was three years. Readers in one study were all members of a special class for children with mild intellectual disability (Love and VanBiervliet, 1984) and in another, readers were all members of a semi-residential programme for children with behavioural and learning difficulties (O'Connor, Glynn & Tuck 1987). Reported reading age gains across the twelve studies reviewed in 1985 ranged from between one-and-a-half and two months per year of trained tutoring to between ten and eleven months per month of trained tutoring. Particularly strong gains were reported for three of the studies in which Pause, Prompt and Praise was introduced concurrently at

home and at school (McNaughton et al.,1981; Scott & Ballard, 1983) or
concurrently in residential and school settings. (O'Connor, Glynn & Tuck,
1984)

One of the earlier evaluations of parent tutoring was undertaken by Jeanne
Biddulph (1983) in seven Christchurch schools. She designed a simple low-cost
parent tutoring programme to enable parents to help low progress nine- and
ten-year-olds. Parents attended four evening sessions and learned strategies
for helping their children, including the Pause, Prompt and Praise method.
Post-tests given seven weeks after the final workshop showed encouraging
gains in reading comprehension, attitudes and reading habits, as well as
improved family relationships, following the tutoring sessions.

Peer tutoring

There may be times when parents will not act as tutors, often in the mistaken
belief that they cannot learn the necessary skills to help their children. Pause,
Prompt and Praise has also been implemented using peers as tutors. Peer
tutors are readily available in schools and their work can be monitored by
teachers. Peer tutoring has also been shown to benefit both the tutor and the
tutee. Helping someone to improve in reading often has a beneficial effect on
the tutor's own reading.

Medcalf and Glynn (1987) taught three primary teachers the Pause, Prompt
and Praise techniques. The teachers in turn taught the techniques to three 11 to
12 year old children who had reading deficits of between one to three years.
The tutors then used the techniques to teach another three eleven- and twelve-
year-olds who had reading deficits of between four and six years. Glynn
describes the results:

> *After eight weeks of tutoring, there were substantial gains for both tutors and*
> *tutees on an informal prose reading inventory, and on the number of successive*
> *book levels read to criterion. The order of gains among the three readers*
> *matched that of their three tutors. The pair making the lowest gains was the*
> *pair who completed the fewest tutoring sessions. (1987:116)*

Medcalf carried out a further study in 1989 with ten subjects, three of whom
acted as tutors for three children while the remaining four used a tape-assisted
reading programme. At the end of the programme the mean gain for the Pause,
Prompt and Praise children was 2.5 years while the children on the tape-
assisted programme made only 1.4 years. Another study by Houghton and
Glynn in 1992 used five pairs of thirteen-year-old children, all of whom were
below average readers. Both tutors and tutees made major gains in reading
accuracy and comprehension.

In another study of peer tutoring in Christchurch schools, Terry Martin (1991)
used the Pause, Prompt and Praise procedures with a 'multi-level' text to help

slow progress eight- and nine-year-olds. The text consisted of 140 tailor-made high-interest reading booklets classified into fourteen 'stairs' of reading difficulty. The tutors, who were competent readers from the same class, and the tutees who were at least two years behind in their reading levels, read in alternating sequence, those sections of the text designed for each. The tutor read the harder sections, the tutee the easier ones. After sixteen weeks the target group of tutees were found to have made a total of sixteen months gain on two prose inventories and improvement continued at a similar rate in the subsequent year. Comparable improvements were noted in the children's attitudes and their book choices.

These studies suggest that as well as being an effective programme for parents to use with their children, there is value in using peers. Furthermore, there is obviously merit in selecting as tutors children who themselves are having difficulties, teaching them the techniques and getting them to tutor other children who are also having difficulties. Glynn (1992) speculates that such tutoring can be seen as a 'responsive social context in which two learners can operate around a common task. It is not a context where expert instructs novice.' (1992:15)

Comparison of Reading Recovery and Pause, Prompt and Praise

Both of these programmes are home-grown New Zealand developments. Both have a substantial and well-documented research base. Neither programme considers it should replace a regular class programme. They both have similar aims — to make children independent readers, able to function in the classroom without additional help. Both have detailed evidence of their success. They differ in the age that they target — Clay considers that age six is an optimum time to intervene if children are making unsatisfactory progress whereas Pause, Prompt and Praise, while not specifying an optimum age, is aimed at older children. They both also avoid labelling children or examining psychological processes. Both start from where the children are at, and focus on reading and language tasks rather than psychological testing. They do reflect the different branches of educational psychology their proponents come from. Clay describes herself as a cognitive psychologist and is concerned with the way the child's information is processed. Glynn's work is grounded in behavioursim and is concerned with the effects of different kinds of reinforcement on children's behaviour.

The biggest difference lies in the contrasting views of who is best suited to help a child having difficulties with reading. Clay considers that experienced teachers who have undergone additional training in Reading Recovery teaching techniques are the only people who can carry out her programme. Glynn considers that a wide range of people — parents, peers and children having reading difficulties themselves — can be successfully taught Pause, Prompt and Praise techniques and can in turn help children having difficulties in reading. The programme has recently been translated into the Maori language and has been presented at a hui (a meeting) for Maori staff of the New Zealand Special Educational Service. The procedures are available to assist children in bilingual units or Kura Kaupapa Maori who are learning to read in Maori.

Clay's particular contribution lies in the fine-grained analysis of reading and the constant monitoring of progress that is at the heart of Reading Recovery. Glynn has shown the professional world of teachers that they do not have a monopoly on the skills of teaching people to read. His procedures are easy to learn and implement and may have value in tutoring in a range of academic subjects.

Although these programmes have different emphases we should see them not in opposition to each other but as different techniques teachers should be familiar with. Both throw light on the reading process and both can enhance the learning of those children who, for whatever reason, are experiencing difficulty in learning to read.

Chapter 13

Conclusion: Another look at reading theory

This book was designed to explain the basis for New Zealand school reading programmes. We have seen how children are initiated gradually into the reading process, by parents' interactions with their young children, in speaking, in story reading and in encouraging a positive attitude towards books. We have seen how primary teachers build on these early accomplishments by means of more regular story reading aloud, shared reading, language experience and regular writing. With such a rich immersion in written language, five-year-olds gradually acquire the fundamental skills of meaning-construction from text as a result of regular practice with interesting repetitive stories and rhymes, by writing about their personal and collective experiences, and by being stretched into a wider range of more and more difficult texts under the guidance of sympathetic adults. With regular practice under non-threatening conditions they teach themselves a range of strategies for working their way through text — responding to such cues as initial and final letters, word shapes, recurrent spelling patterns, syntactic markers, visual aids and the meaning they have constructed so far. This way they learn to read with minimal input from the text, predicting and confirming and making sense as they go. For most children, it is a challenging and enjoyable experience.

We have seen too, how teachers expand children's horizons by promoting and discussing a wide range of good children's literature, and assisting them to improve their comprehension. Above all, we believe that children need to see reading as a pleasant, functional, meaning-getting task — something which they will want to continue to use in later life.

This approach to the teaching of reading, while allowing for a diverse set of strategies, is often referred to as a 'whole language' or 'natural language' approach. It is more 'top-down' than 'bottom-up', as we described in Chapter 7, although there is clearly an interaction of many processes. The focus is on meaning from the start, in both reading and writing, rather than regular, systematic drills and artificial exercises. When New Zealand children are taught new letter-sound links or common blends, this is usually done in the context of a sentence or story. Few teachers design lessons to teach the letter 'p', or the blend 'or', or the effect of adding 'e' to 'at'. They may teach these points incidentally in a shared reading session, or through a handwriting lesson, or in a writing conference. They may ask a group to think of other words that start with 'p', or that end with '-ate'. But it is widely believed that teaching phonic rules explicitly as ends in themselves is a difficult, unnecessary and largely fruitless activity, creating distorted ideas about the nature and purpose of reading. Moreover, children's forgetting of such rules is rapid, and transfer to new words is very difficult for five-year-olds. There is a strong faith that children will work out the rules for themselves, just as they did in oral language.

Children learn much from regular, motivated reading.

In this respect, New Zealand teachers differ considerably from those in other countries. The teaching of reading in most education systems has long been based on the deliberate and systematic teaching of phonic and syntactical rules. Teachers set out to develop phonological awareness, to isolate sounds and letters, and to build up associations between them with regular practice in workbooks and artificial oral exercises and contrived games. Indeed, many children appear to enjoy and see point in some of these exercises. Such activities may be undertaken alongside a more meaning-oriented programme, but usually they precede them. These theoretical differences have given rise to fierce debate in many places and it is fitting to reconsider some of these issues in the final chapter of this book.

Criticisms of whole language approaches

Numerous critics have attacked the basis of the whole language philosophy (eg, Groff, 1980; Vellutino, 1991); others have pointed to the lack of empirical evidence supporting it (Stahl and Miller, 1989; Stanovich, 1992; Chall, 1983); others again have undertaken studies which appear to undermine it (Gough et al, 1980; Nicholson, 1991; Byrne and Fielding-Barnsley, 1991). Teachers need to be aware of the issues raised by these writers and be prepared to defend their own position in the face of criticism from parents, employers and reading specialists with different orientations.

Amongst the most common objections raised against a whole langauge philosophy are the following:

1   Research on eye movements of skilled readers shows that they fixate on almost every word in a text. (Just & Carpenter, 1987) They do not appear to predict, sample and confirm as top-down theorists suggest.

However, this evidence is not conclusive. The extent to which readers process each word is not revealed by such studies. Readers may note only the initial letter, word shape, or syllables at the end of the word. They may also behave differently when their eye movements are being photographed and they know they are being observed.

2   Guessing and predicting strategies are successful only about 25 per cent of the time in normal prose, according to studies done with proficient adult readers (Gough et al, 1980). Therefore it is a waste of time to teach children prediction skills.

It is true that we cannot guess the next word exactly in a text, when it is suddenly covered over. English is not that redundant. However, we can usually reduce the alternatives and come close to predicting the likely meaning of the next word, which makes it unnecessary to do more than glance at the first letters or the shape. Whole language theorists claim that we predict meanings, not exact words. Prediction is very important in reducing the alternative meanings and making our reading more efficient and more meaningful.

3   Skilled readers make very little use of context, because the word identification process is highly automatised. So teaching children to make predictions and sample the print is less efficient than practising decoding from the start. Many studies have shown that weaker readers are more dependent on context than good readers are. (Stanovich, 1992.)

It is true that experimental studies show that as children mature they seem to be able to read words just as well out of context as in context (Nicholson, 1991). However, we know that good readers have had more practice, and have therefore learned to do it either way, depending on their purpose. When reading aloud (as most of these experiments require) the premium is perceived to be on achieving accuracy, so they naturally respond to every word, decoding quickly and accurately; when reading silently they can and do make greater use of context. Moreover, studies of good readers' miscues during running records show that most do make sense in the context. For instance, in a study of 12 000 miscues, undertaken by Rousch & Cambourne (1978), it was found that good and poor readers make similar proportions of grapho-phonically acceptable miscues (20–30 per cent) on suitably graded reading passages. However, good readers make far more semantically acceptable miscues (70 per cent) than poor readers do (35 per cent). Apparently, poor readers are focussing less on meaning and more on the visual cues, which probably slows them down, and takes up too much of their attention as they read. It must be conceded, however, that all these studies of children reading aloud cannot give us final answers on how they read silently, when they are not observed and tested.

4 Learning to read is not a natural act like learning to speak. Rather, it requires specific tuition, and recognition that sounds are represented by letters (Liberman & Liberman, 1990).

It is true that some children experience great difficulty in learning to read, whereas virtually all children do learn to speak. However, if children are immersed in high-interest print, and given real purposes for learning to read it and write about it, they will acquire by themselves the understanding that sounds are represented by letters, and learn these letter-sound links along with the other cues for meaning. Specific tuition about letters and sounds may help some children when they read, but it may also convey wrong impressions about the difficulty and the purposes of reading. And time spent on developing children's ability to sound out as they learn to read may also be counter-productive for later silent reading. Many adult readers still lip-read and/or read aloud under their breath as they read silently. We know that many children do learn to read at home, without systematic tuition (Clark, 1976; Durkin, 1976). We know too that it is possible for readers to go directly from print to meaning, without lessons on sounding out. Thousands of semantically acceptable miscues confirm this fact. When children read 'house' for 'home', or 'Mother said' for 'said Mother', they are clearly going straight from print to meaning, and *then* formulating the sound. Laboratory studies confirm, too, that there is a dual route from words to meaning, sometimes through sound, and sometimes direct (Rayner & Pollatsek, 1989; Crystal, 1994).

5 Most poor readers are deficient in alphabetic coding and phonic awareness (Vellutino, 1991). This is where graphic teaching should be focused, not on prediction and incidental learning.

It is not surprising that poor readers are lacking in decoding skills, as they have usually had very little practice on their own with such skills. However, such children are also deficient in book concepts, prediction skills and deriving meaning from context, to name a few other strategies. All these various skills and strategies will improve with repeated practice, using patterned high-interest materials, and with teacher or peer guidance where needed. Most New Zealand children have learned to read this way. To focus on decoding exercises, outside a meaningful context, is to run the risk of diverting the child's attention away from real reading and from developing other productive strategies.

6   Several research studies have shown that it is possible to teach preschool children phonological awareness, and that this improves their word-recognition skills later (Byrne & Fielding-Barnsley, 1991; Foorman et al, 1991). Such studies show the benefits of structured systematic teaching of letter-sound relationships with many children.

While it may be possible to achieve these outcomes, it is not necessarily desirable. Children usually learn much of what they are taught, especially with novel programmes taught by specialists. The payoff comes in later years when the key components are tested, when comprehension of meaningful prose and attitudes to reading and writing are assessed. Also, comparative studies of reading methods cannot be conclusive, as we rarely know what the experimental groups are being compared with and what other skills and attitudes the control groups are learning — which are not assessed. Studies conducted with six-year-olds, or in countries with predominantly 'bottom-up' approaches, may not be generalisable to New Zealand type situations where reading begins at five, and where high-interest methods such as language experience, shared reading, and creative writing with conferencing are in regular use. We suggest that structured programmes which ignore the crucial role of children's interest will have only a short-term payoff.

7   Some critics argue that whole language proponents have never produced hard evidence, based on standardised test results, to show that their approach is effective in producing competent readers (Stahl & Miller, 1989). Summaries of many comparative studies conducted for the most part in the United States tend to show that 'code oriented' emphases produce better results than 'meaning-oriented' methods (Chall, 1983). Where is the contrary evidence?

Such reviews have to be considered cautiously, and some reading researchers reject them outright, for using irrelevant criteria or for making unfair comparisons (eg, Carbo, 1990). It is important to note that contrast programmes used in United States studies rarely have the kind of components found in New Zealand schools. It is true too, that many are evaluated on very restricted criteria, such as word recognition or tests of phonological skills or artificial exercises. American standardised tests, in the early grades, do stress decoding skills. Whole language teachers usually aim for a much broader range of outcomes. Nevertheless the claim that hard evidence is lacking on the benefits of whole language methods, such as those used in New Zealand, can be rejected in the light of several surveys and empirical studies.

1   New Zealand children who, typically, learn by whole language methods, consistently achieve at very high levels in international studies of reading and literature interpretation (Elley, 1992; Purves, 1973; Thorndike, 1973). In the 1990 IEA survey on formal reading comprehension tests New Zealand had the most high-achieving fourteen-year-olds. While New Zealand children had significantly lower means that Finnish children, they did show the highest average scores of the English-speaking countries.

It is hard to believe that the methods that New Zealand teachers use are not effective. It is true that some have not developed competence this way, but they tend to come from ESOL backgrounds and bookless homes.

2 Singapore children also scored at high levels in the recent IEA study (Elley, 1992) despite their relatively low levels of economic and social development, and despite the fact that they learn to read and write in a non-native language. The distinctive feature of their early programmes is that they too learn by language experience, shared reading and immersion in high-interest print. When comparisons were conducted in Singapore of this style of programme and more structured phonic programmes, the former proved consistently better. (Elley, 1991)

3 A series of empirical studies conducted in the United States by Lesley Morrow (1989, 1990, 1992) have shown extensive benefits for many of the features of whole language programmes. For instance, in one study (Morrow, 1992) the progress of nine United States Grade 2 classes was studied in a literature-based programme which provided a rich literary environment, regular story reading by teachers, with discussion, and lots of self-directed independent reading and writing. The theoretical rationale drew on the work of Holdaway (1979), Cambourne (1988) and Teale (1984), all proponents of whole language approaches. Morrow found substantial increases, relative to control groups, in story comprehension, oral retellings, written retellings, oral and written creation of stories, diversity of vocabulary use, and complexity of sentences. The literature based programme also provided more positive attitudes in pupils, and led to more voluntary book reading. These are important benefits which persuaded the teachers, initially sceptical, to continue with the literature based programme.

4 Many of the component features of the whole language programmes have been evaluated separately using standardised tests, and have been found to produce strong results. For example:

Shared reading: This method, when used with high-interest reading materials proved very effective in promoting reading comprehension, word recognition and oral language in a Nuie study (Elley, 1980; De'Ath, 1980) and in promoting reading, listening, writing, vocabulary and grammar in the Fiji Book Flood study (Elley and Mangubhai, 1983). It also produced positive attitudes and better reading test scores in a New Zealand survey (Elley, 1985).

Silent reading: Empirical studies of the benefits of silent reading for improving achievement in reading are increasing — for examples, see Anderson et al (1988); Stanovich (1992); Taylor et al (1990); and Krashen (1988). The IEA survey (1992) also showed that countries which allocate more time to silent reading produced better test results, other things being equal. Also, recent studies of the extent of exposure to print show promising correlations with achievement (Stanovich, 1992). The Fiji Book Flood, and several other studies of regular exposure to books produced similarly encouraging findings about the important benefits of regular silent reading. Nagy et al (1985) and Jenkins et al (1984) have also demonstrated the vocabulary gains which follow from silent reading.

Story Reading Aloud: Whole language supporters usually emphasise the important role of story reading to children. Holdaway (1979) has spelled out a number of benefits; Durkin (1976) and Clark (1976) show that early readers are much read to at home; Wells (1986) showed substantial benefits of story reading in his longitudinal studies; Cohen (1968) found that American children who were read to improved their language skills; Elley (1989) showed that reading to children enhances vocabulary development in seven- and eight-year-olds; Morrow(1992) found that at-risk kindergarten children benefit considerably from regular story reading, while studies in Israel (Feitelson et al 1986, 1993), Newfoundland (Philips et al, 1990), and Fiji (Ricketts, 1982) found story reading helped improve children's reading. While the practice is widely adopted and has been extensively studied (Doake, 1981; Mason, 1992; Phillips & McNaughton, 1990), it is only recently that empirical studies have shown its benefits in terms of improved achievement results.

Merely reading to children, without discussion, may not of course be so beneficial, but observations of typical story reading sessions show that most teachers use these sessions as an opportunity for productive talk (eg, Altwerger et al 1985; Mason, 1992; McNaughton, 1990; Teale and Sulzby, 1987).

In other words, what appears to some critics as a form of entertainment, with little serious payoff, turns out to be a key ingredient for attracting children to books and for developing their language and meaning-getting strategies. Indeed, the ability to imagine events and things from verbal cues alone, without the concrete image, is fostered by regular story reading. This skill of decontextualising is surely a crucial ingredient in children's development, and enhances their potential for coping with many classroom activities. The child who is restricted to the present concrete image will be seriously handicapped at school.

Conclusion

The last word has clearly not been said in the debates about the relative merits of phonic-based and whole language methods in learning to read. The definitive, conclusive research study is clearly difficult to design and carry out. Most teachers attempt to avoid the extreme positions and artificial constraints of many of the experimental studies conducted. Capturing the role of children's interest in an experimental design is also problematical, yet interests clearly play a key role in the whole language approach.

New Zealand reading methods developed largely as a result of good practice on the part of competent teachers, rather than the accumulation of research findings. Experienced teachers, who observe closely a wide range of children, with various backgrounds, strengths and weaknesses, try out many different approaches and settle on those which seem to work — in terms of children's rates of progress and positive attitudes.

The whole language philosophy allows for a variety of methods, and recognises that different children learn by different approaches. Some children do focus more on visual cues in the early stages, some on meaning and some on syntax. The best mix of these various emphases cannot be universally prescribed. Indeed, there are surely many royal roads to competent reading, and good teachers can make most methods work well.

Nevertheless, we are confident that teachers who immerse their children in high-interest, meaningful literacy tasks; who encourage regular independent reading and writing, and lots of talk about it; who capture and hold their children's inherent interest in a good story, and use that interest to extend the child's knowledge, language and imagination — such teachers will continue to produce future generations of competent readers.

Bibliography

Alton-Lee, A., & Nuthall, G., 1991, 'Pupil Experiences and Pupil Learning in the Elementary Classroom', Teaching and Teacher Education, vol. 6, no. 1, pp. 27-46

Altwerger, A., Diehl-Faxon, J., & Dockstader-Anderson, K. 1985, 'Read-aloud events as meaning construction', Language Arts, vol. 62, pp. 476–84

Anderson, R., Wilson, P., & Fielding, L. 1988, 'Growth in reading and how children spend their time out of school', Reading Research Quarterly, vol. 53, pp. 285–303

Arvidson, G.L. 1960, Alphabetical Spelling List, New Zealand Council for Educational Research, Wellington

Ashby, P. 1986, Funding of Secondary School Libraries, unpublished document, National Library, Invercargill

Ashton-Warner, S. 1963, Teacher, Bantem Books, New York

Ausubel, D. 1963, The Psychology of Meaningful Verbal Learning, New York

Ballard, K. 1980, 'The Questionable IQ — Its conservative effects on Teaching Methods', Education, vol. 29, no. 6, pp. 10–13

Bardsley, D. 1991, Factors Relating to the Differential Reading Attitudes, Habits and Interests of Adolescents, Research Affiliate Report, Education Department, Massey University

Beaglehole, D. 1982, 'Research: The Maori in the School Journal: 1907–1981', Education, vol. 31, no. 1, pp. 38–42

Begg, J.A. & Clay, M. 1968, 'A note on teaching a preschooler to read: some problems of evaluation', New Zealand Journal of Educational Studies, vol. 3, no. 2, pp. 171–174

Benton, N. 1989, 'Education, Language Decline and Language Revitalisation: The Case of Maori in New Zealand', Language and Education, vol. 3, no. 2, pp. 65–81

Biddulph, F. & Biddulph, J. 1993, The Challenge of Non-Fiction, paper presented to Canterbury Reading Association 19th Reading Conference

Biddulph, L. J. 1983, A Group Programme to Train Parents of Children with Reading Difficulties to Tutor their Children at Home, MA thesis, unpublished, University of Canterbury, Christchurch

Bissex, G. 1980, *Gyns at Work: A Child Learns to Read and Write*, Harvard University Press, Cambridge, Mass.

Bormuth, J.R. 1969, 'Factor Validity of Cloze tests as Measures of Reading Comprehension Ability', *Reading Research Quarterly*, vol.4, pp.358-65

Bourke, S. & Keeves, J. 1976, 'Literacy and Numeracy in Australian Schools', *ACER Newsletter*, no.27, pp.1-3

Brown, R. 1973, *A First Language: the early stages*, Harvard University Press, Cambridge, Mass.

Butler, D. 1977, 'Cushla and her books', *Signal*, January, p. 3–5

Buxton J. 1993, 'Daylight Saving Time', *School Journal*, pt 2, no. 2, pp. 2–10

Byrne, B. & Fielding-Barnsley, R. 1991. 'Evaluation of Programme to Teach Phonemic Awareness to Young Children', *Journal of Educational Psychology*, vol.83, pp.451-455

Caddick, A. 1992, *Ethnic and Cultural Representation in School Journals*, Research Report no. 92–4, Education Department, University of Canterbury, Christchurch

Cairney, T.H. 1990, *Teaching Reading Comprehension*, Open University Press, Milton Keynes, UK

Cambourne, B. 1988, *The whole story: National Learning and the acquisition of literacy in the classroom*, Ashton Scholastic, New York

Carbo, N. 1988, 'Debunking the Great Phonics Myth', *Phi Delta Kappan*, Nov., pp.226-40

Cazden, C. 1988, *Interactions Between Maori Children and Pakeha Teachers*, Auckland Reading Association, Council of New Zealand Reading Association, Auckland

Chall, J. 1983, *Stages of Reading Development*, McGraw-Hill, New York

Chamberlain, J. 1993, 'Our Illiteracy: Reading the Writing on the Wall', *North & South*, June, pp. 66–76

Chomsky, C. 1972, 'Stages in language development and reading exposure', *Harvard Educational Review*, vol. 42, no. 1, pp. 1–34

Clark, M.M. 1976, *Young Fluent Readers*, Heinemann Educational Books, London

Clay, M. 1975, *What Did I Write?* Heinemann Educational Books, Auckland

— 1985, 'Engaging with the School System: A study of the interactions in New Entrant Classrooms', *New Zealand Journal of Educational Studies*, vol. 15, no. 2, pp. 137–56

—1985, *Third Edition: The Early Detection of Reading Difficulties*, Heinemann, Auckland

— 1987, 'Implementing Reading Recovery: Systematic Adaptations to an Educational Innovation', *New Zealand Journal of Educational Studies*, vol.22, pp.35-58

— 1987, 'Learning to be Learning Disabled', *New Zealand Journal of Educational Studies*, vol. 22, no. 2, 1987

— 1991, *Becoming Literate: The Construction of Inner Control*, Heinemann Education, Auckland

Cohen, D. 1968, 'The Effect of Literature on Vocabulary and Reading Achievement', *Elementary English*, vol.45, pp.209-13

Crump, B. 1976, 'Early Reading: The Coral Island', *Education*, vol. 9, p. 27

Crystal, D. 1994, 'The Process of Reading', *Set*, no.1, item 9

Dacre, C. 1992, A toddler's shared book experiences, unpublished research study, Dunedin College of Education, Dunedin

De'Ath, P. 1980, 'The shared book experience and ESL', *Directions*, vol. 4, Fiji, pp. 13–22

Department of Education 1972, *Reading Suggestions for Teaching Reading in Primary and Secondary Schools*, Wellington

Department of Education 1985, *Reading in Junior Classes*, Department of Education, Wellington

Doake, D. 1981, Book Experience and Emerging Reading Behaviour, PhD thesis, University of Alberta, Edmonton

Dole, J., Duffy, G., Rochler, L. & Pearson, D. 1991, 'Moving from the Old to the New: Research on Comprehension Instruction', *Review of Educational Research*, vol. 61, no. 2, pp. 239–64

Doman, G. 1964, *Teach your Baby to Read: The Gentle Revolution*, Pan Books, London

Downing, J. & Leong, C.K. 1982, *The Psychology of Reading*, McMillan, New York

Durkin, D. 1976, 'A six year study of children who learned to read in school at the age of four', *Reading Research Quarterly*, vol. 10, pp. 9–61

Durkin, D. 1978, 'What classroom observations reveal about reading comprehension', *Reading Research Quarterly*, vol.14, pp.481-533

Eeds, M. & Wells, D. 1989, 'Grand Conversations: An exploration of meaning construction in literature study groups', *Research in the Teaching of English*, vol. 23, pp. 4–29

Elley, W. B. 1985, *Lessons Learned About Laric*, University of Canterbury, Christchurch

— 1989, 'Vocabulary acquisition from listening to stories, *Reading Research Quarterly*, vol. 24, no. 2, pp. 176–86

—1991, 'Acquiring Literacy in a Second Language: The Effect of Book-Based Programs', *Language Learning*, vol. 41, no. 3, pp. 375–411

— 1992, *How in the World do Students Read?*, International Association for the Evaluation of Education Achievement(1EA), The Hague

Elley, W. B. & Croft, A. C. 1989, *Assessing the Difficulty of Reading Materials: The Noun Frequency Method*, rev. edn, New Zealand Council for Educational Research, Wellington

Elley, W.B. & Mangubhai, F. 1983, 'The Impact of Reading on Second Language Learning', *Reading Research Quarterly*, vol. 9, no. 1, pp. 53–67

Elley, W.B. & Tolley, C. 1972, *Children's Reading Interests*, New Zealand Council for Educational Research, Wellington

Feitelson, D., Goldstein, Z., Iraqi, J. & Shane, D. 1993 'Effects of listening to story reading on aspects of literary acquisition in a dyglossic situation', *Reading Research Quarterly*, vol. 28, no. 1, pp. 70–79

Feitelson, D., Kita, B. & Goldstein, Z. 1986, 'Effects of Reading Stories to First Graders on the Comprehension and Use of Language', University of Haifa, Israel

Ferdman, B.1990, 'Literacy and Cultural Identity', *Harvard Educational Review*, vol. 60, no. 2, pp. 181–203

Ferreiro, E. & Taberosky, A. 1982, *Literacy Before Schooling*, Heinemann, Exeter, New Hampshire

Gambrell, L.B. & Jawitz, P.B. 1993, 'Mental Imagery, Text Illustrations, and Children's Story Comprehension and Recall', *Reading Research Quarterly*, vol.28, no.3, pp.264-76

Gibbons, J. 1980, Benefits of Early Book Experience, M.Ed thesis, unpublished, University of Waikato, Hamilton

Gilroy, A. & Moore, D. 1988, 'Reciprocal Teaching of Comprehension-fostering and Comprehension-monitoring Activities with Ten Primary School Girls', *Educational Psychology*, vol. 8, pp. 41–49

Glynn, T. 1987, 'Effective Learning contexts for exceptional Children', in D.R. Mitchell & N.N. Singh, eds, *Exceptional Children in New Zealand*, Dunmore Press, Palmerston North

Glynn, T., Crooks, T., Bethune, N., Ballard, K. & Smith J. 1989, *Reading Recovery in Context*, Department of Education, Wellington

Glynn, T. & Wheldall, K. 1992, Discussion paper on Pause, Prompt, Praise Reading Tutoring Procedures: Continuing Research and Development, unpublished, University of Otago, Dunedin

Goodman, K. 1976, 'Reading: A Psycholinguistic Guessing Game' in *Theoretical Models and Processes of Reading*, H. Singer & R.B. Ruddell, eds, pp.470-508, International Reading Association, Newark, Delaware

Goodman, K. 1986, *What's Whole in Whole Language*, Heinemann, Portsmouth, New Hampshire

Goodman, K. 1992, 'Why Whole Language is Today's Agenda in Education', *Language Arts*, vol.69, no.5, pp.354-63

Goodman K. & Goodman, Y. 1982, *Reading for Meaning: the Goodman Model*, video of lecture to Australian Reading Association, Sydney

—1983, 'Reading and Writing Relationships: Pragmatic Functions', *Language Arts*, vol. 60, no. 5, pp. 590–99

Goodman, Y. & Burke, C. 1972, *Reading Miscue Inventory: Procedure for Diagnosis and Evaluation*, Macmillan, New York

Gough, P.B. & Hillinger, M.L. 1980, 'Learning to Read: An Unnatural Act', *Bulletin of the Orton Society*, vol.30, pp.179-196

Groff, P. 1990, 'Research versus the Psycholinguistic Approach to Reading', *Elementary School Journal*, vol.81, no. 1, pp.50-55

Haller, E., Child, D. & Walberg, H. 1988, 'Can Comprehension be Taught? A Quantitative Synthesis of Metacognitive Studies', *Education Researcher*, December, pp. 5–8

Halliday, R. 1982, 'A Joy, Not an Obligation', *Education*, no. 1

Harrison, J. 1991, 'Burt's Word Reading Test: Candidate for Retirement', *Reading Forum, New Zealand*, vol.1, pp.23-25

Henson, N. 1991, *Reading in the Middle and Upper School*, Ministry of Education, Wellington

Hill, D. 1993, 'My Dad Drinks', *School Journal*, pt 2, no. 2, pp. 31–35

Hoban, R. 1967, *The Mouse and his Child*, Puffin, Reading

Holdaway, D. 1972, *Independence in Reading*, Ashton Scholastic, Auckland

— 1979, *The Foundations of Literacy*, Ashton Scholastic, Gosford

— 1980, *Independence in Reading*, rev. edn, Ashton Scholastic, Gosford

Ihimaera, W. 1975, 'W. Ihimaera on Plain sailing', *Education*, vol. 24, no. 7, p. 27

Jackson, M. 1979, 'Literacy and Communication' in *Conflict and Compromise: Essays on the Maori since Colonization*, H. Kawharu, ed., A. H. Reed, Wellington

Jenkins, J.R., Stein, M.L. & Wysocki, K. 1984, 'Learning Vocabulary Through Reading', *American Educational Research Journal*, vol.21, pp.767-88

Johnson, F. 1990, *Fourth formers Learning to Learn*, Education Department, University of Canterbury, Christchurch

Just, M. & Carpenter, P.A. 1987, *The Psychology of Reading and Language Comprehension*, Allyn & Bacon, Massachusetts

Kaa, W.M. 1987, 'Policy and Planning: Strategies of the Department of Education in Providing for Maori Language Revival' in *Living Languages: Bilingualism and Community Languages in New Zealand*, W. Hirsch, ed., Heinemann, Auckland

Kelly, M. & Moore, D. 1993, 'I've found my memory', *Set*, no. 2, item 8

Kerslake, J. 1992, 'A Summary of the 1990 Reading Recovery Data', *Bulletin*, no. 5, Research and Statistics Division, Wellington

Kozol, J. 1985, *Illiterate America*, Garden City NY, Anchor Press

Krashen, S.D. 1988, 'Do We Learn to Read by Reading? The Relationship Between Free Reading and Reading Ability' in *Linguistics in Context*, D. Tannen, ed., Ablex

Lamb, H. 1987, *Writing Performance in New Zealand Schools*, Department of Education, Wellington

Liberman, I.Y, & Liberman, A.M. 1990, 'Whole Language Versus Code Emphasis', *Annals of Dyslexia*, vol.40, pp.51-76

Long, S., Winograd, P. & Bridge, C. 1989, 'The effects of reader and text characteristics on reports of imagery during and after reading', *Reading Research Quarterly*, vol.24, no.3, pp.353-72

Luke, A. 1988, *Literarcy, textbooks and ideology: Postwar literary instruction and the mythology of Dick and Jane*, Falmer Press, London

Lunzer, E. & Gardner, K., eds, 1979, *The Effective Use of Reading*, Heinemann, London

McCracken, H., Duncan, S., Leyland, J., Phillips, G., Wade, A. & McNaughton, S. 1985, *Many and Often: Everyday Experiences of Literacy Events in the Lives of Preschoolers*, Education Department, University of Auckland

McDonald G. 1988, 'Promotion, Retention and Acceleration. How the School Promotion Structure Produces Inequalities in the Face of Good Intentions', *Set*, no. 2, item 3

—1991, 'Ten days in new entrant classrooms', *Set*, no. 2, item 14

McKenna, M.C. 1983, 'Informal Reading Inventories: A Review of the Issues', *Reading Teacher*, vol.36, no.7, pp.670-679

McKenzie, D. 1985, *Oral Culture, literacy and print in Early New Zealand: the Treaty of Waitangi*, Victoria University Press, Wellington

McLuhan, M. 1962, *The Gutenberg Galaxy: The Making of Typographic Man*, University of Toronto Press, Toronto

McNaughton, S. 1987, *Being skilled: The socialization of learning to read*, Methuen, London

—1991, What Emerges and Who constructs Children's Development in Literacy, paper presented to the Celebration of Learning Conference, Auckland

McNeill, D. 1966, Developmental Psycholinguistics, in *The Genesis of Language*, F. Smith and G. Miller, eds, MIT Press, Cambridge

Maconie, J. 1984, 'A survey of 6th form Girls' Reading in a Multicultural School', *Set*, no. 1

Marr, M. & Gormley, K. 1982, 'Children's Recall of Familiar and Unfamiliar Text', *Reading Research Quarterly*, vol.18, no.1, pp.90-98

Marriott, R. & Elley, W.B. 1984, *Apprentices Learning in Block Courses*, Christchurch Polytechnic

Martin, T. 1991, *Evaluation of a Cooperative Reading Resource for Low Progress Standard Two Pupils*, Research Report no. 91–2, Education Department, University of Canterbury, Christchurch

Mason, J. 1992, 'Reading Stories to Preliterate children: A Proposed Connection to Reading', in P. Ough, L. Ehri & R. Treiman, eds, Reading Acquisition Lawrence Erlbaum, Hillsdale, New Jersey

Medcalf, J.1989, 'Comparison of peer tutored remedial reading using the Pause, Prompt and Praise procedures with an individualized tape-assisted reading programme', *Educational Psychology*, vol. 9, no. 3, pp. 253–62

Medcalf, J. & Glynn, T. 1987, 'Assisting teachers to implement peer-tutoring remedial reading using pause, prompt and praise procedures', *Queensland Journal of Guidance*, pp.11-23

Meek, M. 1982, *Learning to Read*, Bodley Head, London

Meek, M. 1991, *On Being Literate*, Bodley Head, London

Miller, G. & Gildea, P. 1987, 'How children learn words', *Scientific American*, vol. 257, pp. 94–99

Morris, B. 1986, 'Thinking Through Text' in *Writing and Reading to Learn*, N. Stewart-Dore, ed., Primary English Teachers Association, N.S.W., Australia

Morrow, L.M. 1989, *Literacy development in the early years: Helping children read and write*, Allyn & Bacon, Boston

—1992, 'The impact of a literature-based program on literacy achievement, Use of literature and attitudes of children from minority backgrounds', *Reading Research Quarterly*, vol. 27, no. 3, pp. 250–75

Morrow, L., O'Connor E. & Smith, J. 1990, 'Effects of a story reading programme on the literacy development of at-risk kindergarten children', *Journal of Reading Behaviour*, vol. 22, pp. 255–73

Nagy, W., Herman, P. & Anderson, R. 1985, 'Learning words from context', *Reading Research Quarterly*, vol. 20, pp. 233–53

Nicholson, T. 1984, 'Experts and Novices', *Reading Research Quarterly*, vol. 19, no. 4, pp. 436–50

—— 1986, 'Good Readers Don't Guess', *Set*, no.2, item 13, New Zealand Council for Educational Research, Wellington

—— 1991, 'Do Children Read Words Better in Contexts or in Lists? A Classic Study Re-Visited', *Journal of Educational Psychology*, vol.83, pp.444-50

O'Connor, G., Glynn, T. & Tuck, B. 1987, 'Contexts for remedial reading: Practice reading and pause, prompt & praise tutoring', *Educational Psychology*, vol.7, no.3, pp.207-23

Palinscar, A.S. & Brown A.L. 1984, 'Reciprocal teaching of comprehension-fostering and comprehension monitoring activities', *Cognition and Instruction*, vol. 1, pp. 117–84

Pearson, D. & Fielding, L. 1991, 'Comprehension Instruction' in *Handbook of Reading Research*, vol.2, R.Barr, M. Kamil, P. Mosenthal, & D. Pearson, eds, Longman, New York

Phillips, G. & McNaughton, S. 1990, 'The Practice of Storybook Reading to Preschool Children in Mainstream New Zealand Families', *Reading Research Quarterly*, vol.25, no.3, pp.196-212

Phillips, L., Norris, S., Mason, J. & Kerr, B. 1990, 'Effect of early literacy intervention on linguistic attainment', *Thirty-ninth Yearbook National Library Conference*, Chicago

Pickens, J. & McNaughton, S. 1988, 'Peer Tutoring of Comprehension Strategies', *Educational Psychology*, vol.8, nos.1-2, pp.67-80

Pinnell, G. 1989, 'Reading Recovery: Helping At-Risk Children Learn to Read', *Elementary School Journal*, vol. 90, no. 2, pp. 161-83

Pinnell, G., Lyons, C.A., Deford, D., Bryk, A. & Seltzer, M. 1994, 'Comparing Instructional Models for the Literary Education of High-Risk First Graders, *Reading Research Quarterly*, vol.29, no.1, pp.8-39

Plaister, M. 1993, Memories of Learning to Read, unpublished paper, Dunedin College of Education, Dunedin

Pluck, M., Ghafari, E., Glynn, T. & McNaughton, S. 1984, 'Teacher Modelling of recreational reading', *New Zealand Journal of Educational Studies*, vol. 19, pp. 114–23

Pressley, M., Gaskins, I., Schuder, T., Bergman, J., Almsi, J., & Brown, R. 1992, 'Beyond Direct Explanation: Transactional Instruction of Reading Strategies', *The Elementary School Journal*, vol. 92, no. 5, pp. 513-55

Purves, A. 1973, *Literature Education in Ten countries*, Almquist & Wiksell, Stockholm

—1979, *Achievement in Reading and Literature in the Secondary Schools: New Zealand in an International Perspective*, New Zealand National Centre International Association for the Evaluation of Educational Achievement, Wellington

Rankin, E.F. & Culhane, J.W. 1969, 'Comparable Cloze and Multiple-Choice Comprehension Test Scores', *Journal of Reading*, vol.19, pp.193-198

Rayner, K. & Pollatsek, A. 1989, *The Psychology of Reading*, Prentice-Hall, New Jersey

Reid, N.A. & Elley, W.B. 1991, *Progressive Achievement Tests of Reading*, New Zealand Council for Educational Research, Wellington

Renwick, M. 1984, *To School at Five. The Transition from Home or Pre-School to School*, New Zealand Council for Educational Research, Wellington

Ricketts, J. 1982, 'The Effects of Listening to Stories on Comprehension and Reading Achievement', *Directions*, USP (Suva), vol.8, pp.29-36

Robinson, F.P. 1970, *Effective Study*, 4th edn, Harper & Row, New York

Rogers, R.C. 1994, *The Benefits of Regular Reading: Some Empirical Evidence*, M.Ed thesis, University of Canterbury, Christchurch

Rosenblatt, L. M. 1983, *Literature as Exploration*, 4th edn, Modern Language Association, New York

Rousch, P. & Cambourne, B.L. 1978, A Psycholinguistic Study of the Reading Processes of Proficient Average and Low Ability Readers, Riverina College of Advanced Education, NSW

Royal Commision on Social Policy 1988, *New Zealand Today*, vol. 1

Schon, I., Hopkins, K. & Davis, W. 1982, 'The Effects of Books in Spanish and Free Reading Time on Hispanic Students' Reading Abilities', *National Association of Bilingual Education Journal*, vol.7, pp.13-20

Simpson, M. 1962, *Suggestions for Teaching Reading in Infant Classes*, Department of Education, Wellington

Smith F. 1983, *Essays into Literacy*, Heinemann, New Hampshire

— 1985, *Reading*, 2nd edn, Cambridge University Press, New York

— 1992, 'Learning to Read: the never ending debate', *Phi Delta Kappan*, February, pp. 432-41

Stahl, S.A. & Miller, P.D. 1989, 'Whole Language & Language Experience Approaches for Beginning Reading: A Quantitative Research Synthesis', *Review of Educational Research*, vol.59, no.1, pp.87-116

Stanovich, K.E. 1992, 'The Psychology of Reading: Evolutionary and Revolutionary Developments', *Annual Review of Applied Linguistics*, Cambridge University Press, vol.12, pp.3-30

Stanovich, K.E. & West, R.F. 1989, 'Exposure to Print and Orthographic Processing', *Reading Research Quarterly*, vol.24, no.4, pp.402-33

Stein, N.L. & Glenn, C.G. 1979, 'An Analysis of Story Comprehension in Elementary School Children' in *New Directions in Discourse Processing*, R. Freedle, ed., Ablex Norwood, New Jersey

Sulzby, E. 1985, 'Children's Emergent Reading of Favourite Story Books: A Developmental Study', *Reading Research Quarterly*, vol.20, pp.458-81

Sulzby, E. & Lee, M.O. 1993, 'Children's Emergent Storybook Reading: The Long Transition into Conventional Literacy', *International Journal of Educational Research*, vol.17 pp.1-15

Taylor, B., Frye, B. & Marvgamma, M. 1990, 'Time spent reading and reading growth', *American Educational Research Journal*, vol. 27, pp. 351–62

Taylor, W. L. 1953, 'Cloze Procedure: A New Tool for Measuring Readability', *Journalism Quarterly*, vol. 30, pp. 425–33

Teale, W.H. 1984, 'Reading to Young Children: Its Significance for Literacy Development' in H. Goelman, A. Oberg & F. Smith, eds, *Awakening to Literacy*, Heinemann, London

Teale, W. & Sulzby, E. 1987, 'Literacy Acquisition in Early Childhood: The Roles of Access and Mediation in Storybook Reading', in D. Wagner, ed, *The Future of Literacy in a Changing World*, Pergamon

Terrill, G. 1993, 'The Importance of Oral Language Ability in Literacy Learning', *Reading Forum New Zealand*, vol.3, pp.3-8

Thackery, S., Syme, K. & Hendry, D. 1992, *A Survey of School Entry Practices*, Ministry of Education, Wellington

Tharp, R. & Gallimore, R. 1988, *Rousing Minds to Life: Teaching, Learning and Schooling in Social Context*, Cambridge University Press, Cambridge

Thorndike, R.L. 1973, *Reading Comprehension Education in Fifteen Countries*, Almquist & Wiksell, Stockholm

Tizard, B. & Hughes, M. 1984, *Young Children Learning: Talking and Thinking at Home and at School*, Fontana, London

Tunmer, W. 1990, 'The role of language prediction skills in beginning reading', *New Zealand Journal of Educational Studies*, vol. 25, pp. 95–114

— 1992, 'Phonological Processing and Reading Recovery: a reply to Clay', *New Zealand Journal of Educational Studies*, vol. 27, no. 2, pp. 203–16

Vellutino, F.R. 1991, 'Introduction to Three Studies on Reading Acquisition', *Journal of Educational Psychology*, vol.83, no.4, pp.437-43

Vygotsky, L.S. 1978, *Mind in Society: The Development of Higher Mental Processes*, Harvard University Press, Cambridge, Mass.

Wagemaker, H. 1993, *Achievement in Reading Literacy: New Zealand's Performance in an International Context*, Ministry of Education, Wellington

Waite, J. 1992, *Aoteareo: Speaking for Ourselves*, Part B, Ministry of Education, Wellington

Walmsley, S. & Walp, T. 1990, 'Integrating Literature and Composing into the Language Arts Curriculum: Philosophy and Practice', *The Elemenaary School Journal*, vol. 90, no. 3, pp. 251–74

Wasik, B. & Slavin, R. 1993, 'Preventing Early Reading Failure with One-to-One Tutoring: A Review of Five Programs', *Reading Research Quarterly*, vol. 28, no. 2, pp. 178–200

Wells, G. 1986, *The Meaning Makers: Children Learning Language and using Language to Learn*, Heinemann, Portsmouth

Wheldall, K. & Entwhistle, J. 1988, 'Back in the USSR: the effect of teacher modelling of silent reading on pupils' reading behaviour in the primary school classroom', *Educational Psychology*, vol. 8, nos 1–2, pp. 51–66

Wheldall, K. & Glynn, T. 1989, *Effective Classroom Learning*, Basil Blackwell, Oxford

White, D. 1954, *Books Before Five*, New Zealand Council for Educational Research, Wellington

Wilkinson, I. & Anderson, R. 1992, *Micro-Experimental Analysis of the Small-Group Reading Lesson: Social and Cognitive Consequences of Silent Reading*, Center for the Study of Reading, Champaign, Illinois

Wittrock, M.C., Marks, C.G. & Doctorow, M. 1975, 'Reading as a Generative Process', *Journal of Educational Psychology*, vol.67, pp.484-89

Wong P. & McNaugton, S. 1980, 'The Effects of prior provision of context on the oral reading proficiency of a low progress reader', *New Zealand Journal of Educational Studies*, vol. 15, no. 2, pp. 169–76

Wood, D., Bruner, J.S. & Ross, G. 1976, 'The Role of tutoring in problem solving, *Journal of Child Psychology*, vol.17, pp.89-100.

Wright, A. 1993, 'Evaluation of the First British Reading Recovery Programme', *British Educational Research Journal*, vol.18, no.4, pp.351-68